Lost Trea.
of the Oregon Coast

Theodore Schellhase

Schiffer Publishing Ltd®

4880 Lower Valley Road   Atglen, Pennsylvania   19310

Schiffer Books are available at special discounts for bulk purchases for sales promotions or premiums. Special editions, including personalized covers, corporate imprints, and excerpts can be created in large quantities for special needs. For more information contact the publisher:

Published by Schiffer Publishing Ltd.
4880 Lower Valley Road
Atglen, PA 19310
Phone: (610) 593-1777; Fax: (610) 593-2002
E-mail: Info@schifferbooks.com

For the largest selection of fine reference books on this and related subjects, please visit our web site at **www.schifferbooks.com**
We are always looking for people to write books on new and related subjects. If you have an idea for a book please contact us at the above address.

This book may be purchased from the publisher.
Include $5.00 for shipping.
Please try your bookstore first.
You may write for a free catalog.

In Europe, Schiffer books are distributed by
Bushwood Books
6 Marksbury Ave.
Kew Gardens
Surrey TW9 4JF England
Phone: 44 (0) 20 8392-8585; Fax: 44 (0) 20 8392-9876
E-mail: info@bushwoodbooks.co.uk
Website: www.bushwoodbooks.co.uk
Free postage in the U.K., Europe; air mail at cost.

Contents

Acknowledgments

The efforts of maritime historian, James Gibbs, were a significant source for this book. He wrote *Shipwrecks of the Pacific Coast, Pacific Graveyard,* and *Oregon's Salty Coast.* Don Marshall's *Oregon Shipwrecks* and the books by Bert Webber, including *Amazing True Tales of Wrecked Japanese Junks,* and the treasure stories by Ruby El Hult were important contributing sources.

The accounts of the first explorers into the Oregon Territory contained the early history of Oregon, beginning with journals from men like Alexander Mackenzie, David Thompson, and Lewis & Clark, which led to the founding of Astoria, as described by Astor's Pacific Fur Co. clerks Gabriel Franchere, Alexander Ross and Ross Cox., and concluding with Washington Irving's *Astoria.* The first pioneers wrote of their journeys overland and into Oregon, and described the first encounters with the native people on the coast. They passed on the legends of white-winged ships that first came to these shores, and the eyewitness accounts of survivors from shipwrecks, who intermarried with the local tribes. Warren Vaughn, one of the early pioneer settlers, wrote *Till Broad Daylight,* James Swann wrote *The Northwest Coast,* and the first missionaries into Oregon, Lee and Frost, wrote *Ten Years in Oregon.*

The works of Hubert Howe Bancroft, *History of the Northwest Coast,* aided by his greatest contributor, Frances Fuller Victor, I found to be the most entertaining. The early *History of Oregon* by Charles Carey was an additional guide. Some of the most important works were from the authors Samuel A. Clarke, S. J. Cotton, John Hobson, Thomas Rogers, and James Wickersham, who all contributed to the *Oregon Native Son* between the years 1899 and 1900, a rare publication in the archives of Central Library, in downtown Portland, which also holds the many articles on microfilm from the *Oregonian* and *Oregon Journal.*

The research library at Tillamook County Pioneer Museum and Oregon Historical Society were helpful. Heidi Pierson and the entire staff at Fort Vancouver National Historic Site, and especially the Gresham Library staff, provided vital help.

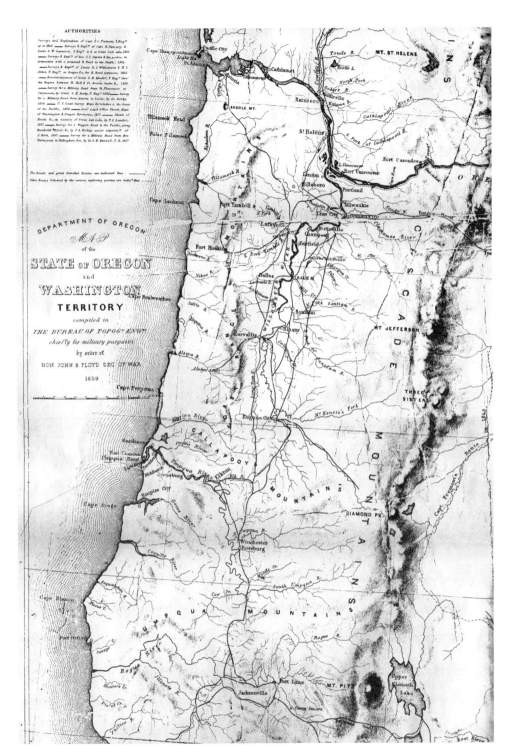

"Map of the State of Oregon and Washington Territory"
compiled by The Bureau of Topog. Eng. 1859.

Introduction

A wooden rigging block was picked up at the mouth of the Nehalem River in Oregon, in 1993, by a beachcomber who almost tossed it in the fire he built on the beach. Fortunately, he took it to the Columbia River Maritime Museum, where Jerry Ostermiller, Executive Director, could tell immediately that it was a rigging block from a Spanish galleon from the late 16th or early 17th century. A maritime expert in Madrid later confirmed his findings. A piece of the block was sent to the University of Washington, where it was tested in the High-precision Radiocarbon Laboratory. The test returned a date of 1632, which also closely matched the carbon-test dates for the beeswax, a ship's pulley, and a teak cane, all believed to be from the same wreck.

Teakwood was used in the construction of Spanish galleons and Oriental junks, and has been collected in great quantities on the Nehalem beaches. The pulley was recovered from the hull of the ship exposed in the sand, during an extremely low tide in 1896. It was also made of teak and was carbon-dated to the mid-1600s. Just two years later, in 1898, another very important artifact, a silver reliquary, was removed from the hull of the shipwreck, then showing two masts jutting up from its remains.

Beeswax has been found in the sands of Nehalem since the early nineteenth century, and was carried on the decks of the galleons from Manila, as well as cargo on the Oriental junks. The Nehalem beeswax was carbon-dated to 1681, by Shell Oil Company Laboratories in 1961.

Archaeological excavations conducted in the Nehalem and Tillamook Bay areas have turned up Chinese porcelain shards and even arrowheads made from these pieces. In addition to the surprising porcelain discoveries, archaeologists found Chinese coins and beeswax at sites that were worked in the mid-1950s.

Shipwreck survivors, who married into Indian tribes on the Oregon coast, and eyewitnesses of the events were the source of the accounts of the white-winged ships. Explorers Meriwether Lewis and William Clark met one descendent of the castaways at Fort Clatsop in 1805, and the same young man, with his name tattooed on his left arm, was seen again at Astoria in 1813.

There have been more than sixty junks found adrift or wrecked in the Pacific ocean from the earliest recordings up to 1875. One junk is known to have wrecked on Clatsop Beach, just south of Point Adams in 1820, and another near Cape Flattery in 1833.

Spanish galleons crossed the Pacific for over 250 years, from 1565 until 1815. They sailed between Manila in the Philippines and Acapulco in New Spain (now Mexico). The ships were laden with the wealth of the Orient: gold, silk, porcelain, ivory, spices, and beeswax. There were at least forty galleons that were shipwrecked or reported lost along the galleon route, and one of these lies in the sands of the Nehalem shore.

Spanish Galleons
Sir Francis Drake

Sir Francis Drake captured the Spanish treasure ship *Nuestra Senora de la Concepcion*, off the coast of Equador, in 1578. He removed an incredible amount of loot from the galleon, including gold, silver, emeralds, silks, and even spices. He withdrew 80 pounds of gold, 13 chests of gold plate, and 26 tons of silver. So much was taken from the Spanish vessel, that his ship, the *Golden Hind* became seriously overloaded, forcing him to heave a portion overboard. He also relieved the captain of his charts & logs, which revealed the route of the Manila galleons to the Philippines. Drake may have happened upon a copy of the *Padron Real*, a master chart, with the original closely guarded in Seville.

Drake seized another Spanish ship, bound for Panama, near Costa Rica, and the ship's charts, with two pilots, who had experience on the Acapulco-Manila run. These charts and sailing directions, and the personal knowledge of the pilots, gave Drake and other British captains these secrets, now unknown to their Spanish counterparts. The ship was laden with China silk and porcelain, and a most handsome piece – a golden falcon, "with a great emerald set in the breast of it."

Drake then sailed northwards along the coast, in search of the Strait of Anian – the fabled Northwest Passage, and a favorable site for an English colony, but we know from the account written by the ship's chaplain, Francis Fletcher, in "The World Encompassed," that he didn't find it:

> And also from these reasons we conjecture, that either there is no passage at all through these northern coasts (which is most likely), or if there be, that yet it is un-navigable. Add hereunto that though we searched the coast diligently, even unto the 48 deg., yet found we not the land to trend so much as one point in any place towards the east, but rather running on continually north-west, as if it went directly to meet Asia…

Spanish Galleons

The captain then headed south along the Pacific coast, until he found a sandy cove to careen his ship, before the long journey home.

Upon Sir Francis Drake's return to England in September 1580, a veil of secrecy was immediately imposed on the expedition. The captain's logs & charts were confiscated by Queen Elizabeth, and the crew was sworn to secrecy, forbidden to speak of the voyage and where they had been, especially during the summer of 1579.

The first official account of the expedition was published in 1589, by Sir Richard Hakluyt, ten years after Drake's return, and places the cove at 38 degrees, Drake's Bay, just north of San Francisco, also noted by Fletcher: "In 38 deg. 30 min. we fell with a convenient and fit harbour, and June 17 came to anchor therein, where we continued till the 23 day of July following." But a journal, discovered in a British museum, known as the "Anonymous Narrative," believed to have been written by a member of the crew, locates them at 44 degrees north latitude, on the Oregon coast:

> Sailing northwards till he came to 48 degrees of the septentrional latitude, still finding a very large sea trending towards the north, but being afraid to spend a long time in seeking for the strait he turned back again, still keeping along the coast, as near land as he might, until he came to 44 degrees and then he found a harborough for his ship where he grounded his ship to trim her...

The Narrative does not say when they were there. The harbor where they anchored, was mapped by Drake and appeared on the 1589 world map by Joducus Hondius, most well-known as the Drake Broadside map. It includes a portrait of Queen Elizabeth and a picture of the *Golden Hind*. The mapmaker shows the bay as "Portus Nova Albionis," an unbelievably accurate depiction of Whale Cove, just south of Depoe Bay, at 44 deg. 44 min.

The map also shows where the ship turned back at 42 degrees

on its northern route, but there are also indications that the track was first marked continuing to about 48 degrees, and was then partially deleted. The "Narrative" and "The World Encompassed" both state that they sailed to 48 degrees north latitude. (Hampden, 1972, pp. 170-176)

Following Drake's return from the successful circumnavigation of the globe, the official policy of secrecy meant that his map was available for viewing by a privileged few. One of these was Sir Robert Dudley, who invested in the expedition, and was also the creator of an atlas, the "Dell Arcano del Mare," from 1647. In a rough drawing he shows a cove opening to the southwest, and protected from northwesterly winds by a small peninsula, just like Whale Cove. The drawing also includes a measurement, in fathoms, indicating a shallow harbor, at New Albion, and Whale Cove is a shallow harbor, whose depths correspond to those readings on Dudley's map.

There have been a number of discoveries authenticating a visit, which predates the eighteenth-century explorers. A ship's cutlass was found in Newport in the nineteenth century, bearing the markings of a 16th century English armory, and an English coin, a "shilling," dated 1560, was discovered on the coast in 1982.

Rotting timbers were uncovered near Whale Cove that may have been a stockade built by Drake's crew. Captain Drake also described native houses near the bay, similar to those partially excavated by a team of archaeologists from Oregon State University, in 1985, on a bluff overlooking Whale Cove. (Bawlf, 2003, 314-316, also see Morris, 2004, 139)

The discovery of five cannons and an anchor in 1981, provides additional evidence that Sir Francis Drake sailed along the Pacific Coast, and through the Santa Barbara Channel. When the *Golden Hind* cruised into its home port, she was missing five cannons and an anchor. On January 21, 1981, a beachcomber came across two rock-encrusted objects, about half a mile east of Goleta Beach Park, California, which turned out to be cannons. He returned the next day and found three more, along a 50 foot area of the beach uncovered during low tide.

Volunteers from the University of California at Santa Barbara's Archaeology and History departments, along with rangers from the County Park Department, hauled the five cannons out of the surf and transported them to the University campus. The United States Navy provided x-ray testing for two of the cannons, that proved to be from a 16th century English design.

Wood-cutters in the area also found a 16th century iron anchor in the mud west of Goleta slough, which was identified as the type of anchor used by the *Golden Hind*. The ancient relic was found at a spring that flowed before the flood of 1861, and was a favorite source of freshwater for Spanish and American ships, to top off their water casks. (Wheeler and Kallman, 1986, 5-7)

English Colony

It is possible that Sir Francis Drake came ashore further north on the Oregon coast, near Neahkahnie Mountain, where a land survey was located in 1968. The news of the discovery was made known by M. Wayne Jensen, Director of the Tillamook County Pioneer Museum, in their publication, "Tales of the Neahkahnie Treasure." Mr. Jensen measured rocks and the distances between them, believing they were survey stones for a colony. Accompanied by Don Viles of Garibaldi, they uncovered a circular platform of stones, about 10 inches in diameter by two feet high, and nearby, a rock with the numerals "1632" inscribed within a triangle, which may have been a date. A mile up the mountain they found another circular platform, and a stone with a groove cut across its surface, (approx 36 inches?) The inscribed numbers were not a date, but a measured distance. They had been following the Spanish measurement – "vara" without finding anything, but after switching to the English "yard" they began locating other inscribed stones, covered by the overgrowth.

"By studying aerial photographs, and the ground, we found that the 1632 carved on Windle's stone represented 1632 yards," said Jensen. "Going north from the south mound it was approximately 1,632 yards to the north mound. A survey was the final conclusion…The theory as to why this was done is a land claim. There has been no recorded survey that we have been able to find." The 1632 stone was first seen in 1947 by Ed Windle, after a fire along the ridge, burned away the overgrowth.

"A drawing of one of the original rocks in 1895 shows the word "Deos" along a side of the "W." The spelling of Deos has only been found in a sketch made by Sir Francis Drake or one of his crewmen of Nombre De Deos, Central America, Drake's drawing was the only place this spelling has been found using an E instead of an I." In 1572, Drake and his men attacked Nombre de Dios, known as the "Treasure City," on the Atlantic side of Panama. The name of the city is spelled with an "I."

While studying "some pictures of the so-called treasure rocks with strange marks engraved on their surfaces," Mr. Viles recalled, "I suddenly realized the engraving represented compass bearings!" They had discovered a plane table triangulation survey made in 1579, by Drake's crew. (Jensen, 1991, 13-18)

While searching for examples of old survey methods, Mr. Jensen and his associates found a drawing by William Bourne, author of "A Regiment For the Sea," of a survey at his home in Gravesend on the Thames River. A survey that Samuel Bawlf, author of "The Secret Voyage of Sir Francis Drake," believed was made to demonstrate the use of triangulation, to measure distances to various landmarks.

Mr. Bawlf also mentioned in his book, that a storm exposed an Elizabethan coin on the beach, somewhere near Neahkahnie Mountain. (Bawlf, 2003, 308-309)

Don Viles completes the investigation by saying: "The Neah-kahnie treasure is Francis Drake's survey with which he claimed for England all land north of 45 degrees North Latitude. Political intrigue kept this fact hidden from the public, but England used same in all her claims to Western North America during later diplomatic negotiations." (Jensen, 1991, 15)

Galleon Shipwrecks

The Spanish galleons operated in the Pacific for over 250 years, from 1565 until 1815. They sailed between Manila, in the Philippines, and Acapulco, in New Spain. The galleons left Acapulco, usually in December, taking eight to ten weeks to arrive in the Islands. After the discovery of the westerly winds in the Pacific between 40 and 44 degrees north, in 1564, the navigators began searching for a route back to Acapulco. In 1565, Andres de Urdaneta successfully proved that the northwest current of Japan would carry a vessel to California.

The crew of a Chinese vessel was rescued by the captain of a Spanish galleon in the Philippines in 1571. The next year, 1572, another Chinese ship arrived in Manila carrying Asian goods, which began a direct trade route with China.

Acapulco became the trading port of the Manila galleons in 1570, because of its excellent harbor, and its access to the overland route to Vera Cruz, on the Caribbean side of Mexico. From there the goods were loaded onto ships of the Nueva Espan fleet, to Havana, and then the return journey to Spain.

The galleons were laden with the wealth of the Orient: silk, porcelain, gold, ivory, gems, jade, and other valuables from the East. There was a great demand in China for Spanish silver from mines in Peru, carried by the westbound galleons, usually 200,000 pesos of silver. Upon arriving in the islands, silver was traded for Oriental silks, cinnamon, beeswax, and Chinese porcelain, for Chinese porcelain was as valuable as gold.

The greatest number of shipwreck losses during the two hundred and fifty year span of the galleon fleet, occurred in or near the Islands. In the *National Geographic* article "Track of the Manila Galleons" the historian Eugene Lyon determined there were at least 40 galleons that were lost at sea or wrecked. The first recorded event was the wreck of the *San Pablo* in the Marianas in 1568. (Lyon, 1990, 18)

The *San Agustin* sailed from Manila with treasure on July 5, 1595, for New Spain, and the port of Acapulco, with a cargo of porcelain, and precious silks. The ship sailed in a northeast direction reaching the north latitude of 35 degrees, and then into the westerly winds that carried it south. The ship arrived near Trinidad Head, 65 miles south of the Oregon-California border, and then continued along the coast to Drake's Bay, just north of San Francisco. While anchored in the bay, she was hit by a ferocious storm, and wrecked on the shore, spilling out her cargo of porcelain, chests of silk, and a quantity of beeswax.

In 1941, and again in 1952, archaeologists from the University of California excavated Indian graves that contained iron rods and metal from the wrecked galleon. They also removed 125 sherds of the Wan Li and Chai Ching blue Chinese porcelain. The estimated value of the ship's cargo was believed to be $500,000.

U. S. Navy divers working in the "Tektite Project" during the late 1960s, exposed an ancient Chinese ship hidden underneath the *San Agustin*, resting on the bottom of Drake's Bay.

The Spanish galleon *Santa Rosa* was wrecked, near San Miguel Island, off the coast of California, in 1717, leaving pieces of beeswax and Chinese porcelain. The galleon carried an estimated $700,000 in gold and silver.

On September 20, 1638, the *Nuestra Senora de la Concepcion*, foundered in the Mariana Islands, with great treasure aboard, and was wrecked on the coast of Saipan. The galleon was loaded with Chinese silks & rugs, porcelain, cotton from India, ivory from Cambodia, camphor from Borneo, and precious jewels from Burma, Ceylon and Siam.

A mutiny arose over control of the ship, when it was mishandled by an inexperienced commander, Don Juan Francisco, the young nephew of Don Sebastian Hurtado de Corcuera, the governor of Manila. An official inquiry into the loss of the ship in 1644, charged the governor with misappropriating the treasures of the islands, and shipping his personal cargo aboard the galleon back to Spain.

The galleon was forced onto Saipan's Agingan Point, after being caught in a storm and hurled onto the reef by tremendous waves, where it was pulverized by coral, spilling its ballast and cargo. The largest portion of the *Concepcion* was found in shallow water, and a section with storage jars was located further out, at depths of 140 to 250 feet.

William M. Mathers was aboard the discovery ship *Tengar* on March 10, 1988, when the "Golden Lady," was found. His accounts were published in "National Geographic" September 1990, in the article *Nuestra Senora de la Concepcion*. The research vessel was the home for a crew of 30 during a two year salvage period. The team recovered over 1300 pieces of jewelry, a few hundred cannon balls, and 156 storage jars.

The storage jars were scattered across the bottom of Saipan's nearby sea, still intact after resting in the sands for over three hundred years. The jars were fired in the kilns of Thailand, China, and Viet Nam. Numerous shards of Ming dynasty porcelain and at least one complete porcelain jar were also recovered. (Mathers, 1990, 40)

Six galleons left Manila for Acapulco, and failed to reach their destination: The *Nuestra Senor del Pilar,* like the *Concepcion*, is believed to have wrecked in the Philippines, off the coast of Luzon, in 1750; the *Santo Cristo de Burgos*, may have been lost in the Marianas, in 1693; the *San Juanillo* was lost in 1578, location unknown; the *San Juan* in 1586, the *San Francisco Xavier*, in 1705, and the *San Antonio* in 1603.

The *San Antonio* left Manila with many wealthy families on board, fleeing the revolution in the Philippines. The ship carried fabulous amounts of personal treasure – millions of dollars in uncut stones, jewelry, cash, gold and silver bullion – the richest cargo of any galleon in two and a half centuries. The galleon, however, never reached its final destination, and was reported missing in 1603.

Beeswax

The *San Francisco Xavier* was built in Cavite, in the Philippines, in 1691, and was the third galleon to be christened with the saint's name. It was spread for a 50 foot beam, 175 feet long, with a 1500 ton cargo capacity, and 60 cannons, four of these guns actually salvaged from the *Concepcion* wreck of 1638. Constructed like other Manila galleons, her frames were of teak and other durable hardwoods, such as lanang and molave.

World traveler, Francisco Gamelli Careri reported from the deck of the overloaded *San Francisco Xavier* in 1697, that the heavy ship was forced to return to port to offload passengers, and a great amount of beeswax. In "Flood Tide of Empire," a study of Spanish explorations, by Warren Cook, the author points out that the *San Francisco Xavier* carried 500 cakes – 75 tons of beeswax when she sailed from Manila, but never reached Acapulco. The galleon was commanded by Santiago Zabalburu, when she sailed from Manila. The beeswax, was valued at 150,000 piasters – pieces of eight or dollars. The additional cargo included 2,000 packs of silks, gold ingots worth, 2,500 piasters, porcelain ware, and spices; the total value of the shipment set at 4,000,000 piasters. (Cook, 1973, 34-35)

Beeswax has been found in the sands of Nehalem beach, since the early nineteenth century. The earliest known reference to beeswax from the Philippines may be from Commodore Byron's "Voyage Around the World." The historian John B. Horner states that: "Commodore Byron, under the date of May 9, 1766, in his "Voyage Around the World" Chapter V, leads us to infer that the wax could have been shipped from Manila."

Dr. C. E. Linton, who was a pharmacist in Waldport, related to Mr. Horner his discovery of beeswax at Nehalem: "While conducting a drug store at Nehalem City in 1892, I collected two tons of beeswax along the shore after a storm, and I sold the product to Woodward & Clark and another firm in Portland, both houses purchasing it as beeswax." (Horner, 1929, 48-55)

Waldemar H. Hollenstead of Portland holds an inscribed beeswax block found on the Nehalem Peninsula by a group of students from MacLaren School, who were planting grass for Oregon State Parks in January 1955. (Ben Maxwell photo. Salem Public Library Historic Photograph Collection)

In the August 1961 issue of "True West" magazine, there is an article by Ben Maxwell entitled, "Messages in Beeswax From a Missing Galleon." In his story he indicated how Spanish galleons were making landfall at Cape Mendicino, northern California, the point in the route used by Manila galleons since 1564, crossing the Pacific to Cape Mendicino, and then turning south to New Spain. This would have been the route taken by the *San Francisco Xavier*. It was a region of great storms and diverse ocean currents – the strong ocean currents flow north and have carried California redwood to the Oregon coast.

The article also explained how the Indians were digging chunks of wax from the beach near the mouth of the Nehalem River, and trading them with Alexander Henry, of the Northwest Company at Astoria. Some of this beeswax made its way to the pioneers at Fort Vancouver.

A new mystery was added to the beeswax story connected with the Nehalem shore, by the discovery of a large chunk of the substance under a stump some distance back from the Tavern at Neah-Kah-Nie. While digging out a stump the men removed a root that was more than two feet thick. Under this root the chunk of wax was found. From all indications the tree must have been several hundred years old and the wax placed or drifted there when the tree was small. (Treasure Hunt Revived" from The Oregonian, March 15, 1915.)

The beeswax block, found by Edmund Halley Lane and his brother Jack in 1905, with the large letter M, was cut open by Ben Lane. To his amazement, he had revealed a hollow compartment, filled with beeswax candles, that still retained the wicks through their centers.

Mrs. Ben Lane adds that a summer resident found a cake that was about five inches thick and weighed approximately 13 pounds, with a four-leaf clover design and two spears crossing the center diagonally.

There was a historical exhibit in the Ben Lane Building at Manzanita in 1938, where a quantity of beeswax was displayed along with a model of a 16th century merchant marine vessel. One visitor to the exhibit was the grandson of J. E. Reeder, an early settler on Sauvies Island, and Mrs. Ben Lane, the writer, added that the Reeder family kept a map showing where a treasure is buried in the vicinity of Nehalem. (Beeswax Observations by Mrs. Ben Lane, Manzanita Beach, January 17, 1938)

The famous treasure hunting author, Ruby El Hult, received a letter from Mrs. Norman P. Allen of Portland, who recalled finding a chunk of beeswax in 1930. Her father discovered a compartment that had been cut into the piece, revealing an aged yellow paper, written in Spanish, or possibly Latin, with the word *Jesu* appearing many times, a page left in the wax, from the Bible, or possibly a personal prayer book. (Hult, 1971, 104)

In the Tillamook County Pioneer Museum there is a large cake of beeswax inscribed with the numbers "67" which many people think is the second and third numerals of the year "1679," and the Nehalem beeswax was radio carbon-dated to 1681, by Shell Oil Company Laboratories in 1961. This piece was discovered on the Nehalem spit, in 1909, and donated to the museum by Mrs. A. C. Anderson. It was originally displayed at the Nehalem Valley Bank.

The entry for the "Beeswax Legend" from the "Dictionary of Oregon History" states that a Clatsop Indian legend says that the beeswax was from a Spanish ship, wrecked on Nehalem Beach, with the blocks weighing approximately 20 pounds, and inscribed with the letters "I.H.S." and "I.H.N," an indication that the shipment was , consigned to the Catholic missions. The ship may have been the *San Jose* which was lost in June, 1769. (Corning, 1989, 25)

In Bancroft's appendix he mentions a wreck "with a cargo of beeswax cast ashore on the northern side of the entrance to the Columbia," from the "Oregon Spectator" Jan. 21, 1847.

Frank J. Kumm in front of the entrance to the Tillamook County Pioneer Museum. June 20, 1952, holding the famous "67" block of bees-wax. A sample from this cake was carbon-dated to 1681, by Shell Oil laboratories in 1961. (Ben Maxwell Photo. Salem Public Library Historic Photograph Collection)

The Sacred Expedition

The Marine Department of San Blas was organized to oversee maritime operations in 1764, and Don Jose de Galvez was appointed to the Council of the Indies. In 1765, he carried the request of the king to Mexico, with instructions to rediscover San Diego, and to occupy it, and other harbors on the coast. An expedition by land and sea, to establish settlements north of New Spain, was initiated. The land expedition was under the command of Gaspar de Portola, with assistance from the President of Missions, Father Junipero Serra, leader of the Franciscans. The second in command was Captain Moncado, who had made a tour of the northern Jesuit missions and gathered together men, provisions, and 200 head of cattle & horses, for the new colonies. The animals were sent overland, from Loreto, after being collected in Baja, while the religious items and agricultural supplies were transported by ship.

The first overland party set out on the 24th of March, accompanied by a Franciscan priest; with 25 soldiers, six packers, a guide, and several herders. They made San Diego on the 14th of May. "The Sacred Expedition," as it became known, was led by Governor Portola, and Father Serra. They left on 15th of May from Velicate, the Spanish settlement in Baja, and arrived on July 1, 1769, at San Diego, after a long six week journey. There they established the first settlement & mission in Upper California.

The ships of the sea expedition sailed from Baja and included three vessels: the *San Carlos,* the *San Antonio* and the *San Jose.* The *San Carlos* and the *San Antonio* had been supplied from San Blas, and were also being equipped for the voyage at La Paz. The ships were to leave at different dates, but the destination for all three was San Diego. The *San Carlos* sailed first, from La Paz on January 9, 1769, with 62 aboard and arrived at San Diego on the First of May. The *San Antonio* followed, a month later, departing from Cabo San Lucas, on the 15th and reached her port on the 11th of April. The third and final vessel the *San Jose,* sailed from La Paz on the 16th of June, but failed to arrive at its destination and was reported missing. (Yenne, 2004, 10 and also Evans, 1889, 29-30)

Trading Vessels
Lewis & Clark

Long before the first white man arrived on the Oregon coast, before the arrival of the Lewis & Clark Expedition, and even before the first English ships explored the northern coast, an Indian from the Louisiana Territory walked among the native inhabitants of Oregon. The explorer was listed in the early "History of Oregon" by the author Charles Carey:

> There was a story of a Yazoo Indian called Moncacht Ape or Moncachtabe, seen in his old age in the lower Mississippi region by a French scholar and writer. This Indian claimed to have visited the Pacific coast in 1745, or about that time, and to have learned there of the regular visits of a ship to that coast, and to have seen bearded visitors... (Carey, 1922, 95 also see Bancroft, 1884, vol. 2, 605)

The adventures of Moncachtape were included in "The History of Louisiana," by Antoine Simon LePage du Pratz, a French military engineer, who came to North America in 1718. In 1758, Du Pratz published his three-volume work, "Histoire de la Louisiane," which was translated to the English in 1763, under the lengthy title "The History of Louisiana, or of The Western Parts of Virginia and Carolina: Containing a Description of the Countries that lie on both Sides of the River Mississippi: With an Account of the Settlements, Inhabitants, Soil, Climate, and Products." His 1774 edition was reprinted in New Orleans by J. S. W. Harmanson, n.d.

The Lewis & Clark Expedition carried a copy of a 1774 English edition of Du Pratz's "History of Louisiana" as well as Mackenzie's "Voyages from Montreal." President Thomas Jefferson kept an edition of Du Pratz's work, and used it as a reference source to prepare his treatise on Louisiana. Meriwether Lewis borrowed an English edition of this book from Benjamin Smith Barton, his botany tutor in Philadelphia, and took it on the expedition to the

Pacific. "A map of Louisiana, with the course of the Mississippi," the title of Du Pratz's map, is included in the first English edition of his publication.

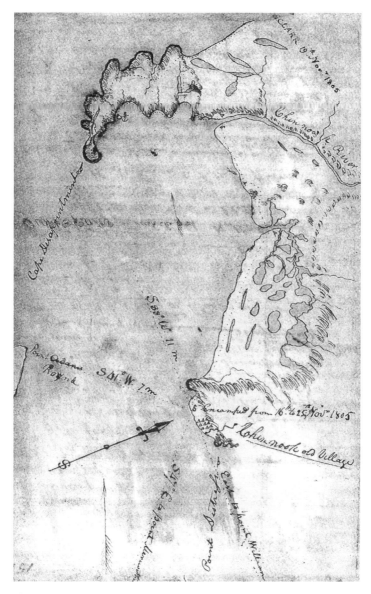

Captain William Clark's map of the mouth of the Columbia River, "19th. Nov. 1805." The anchor indicates the favored bay of the trading vessels.

Trading Vessels

The Lewis & Clark Expedition arrived at the entrance to the Columbia River in November 1805, and were hoping to meet a trading vessel returning to the east coast. One of the journal entries at Fort Clatsop says they were looking for a ship: "It is probable that a vestle will come in this winter," Clark wrote. Although President Thomas Jefferson informed various sea captains, who sailed to the northwest, of the presence of the Expedition, there is no record that any ship's captains searched for the Corps, except for Captain Samuel Hill, of the *Lydia*. The historian Charles Carey said that the *Lydia* was on the Columbia in November of 1805 just two weeks after Lewis & Clark had passed down the river, and missed seeing them.

Scouts were traversing both sides of the great river, searching for a site to build the winter camp. They decided on a southern location, not far from the Columbia, after the scouting party reported seeing more elk in this area. Here they built Fort Clatsop, named after the Indians living nearby. The Clatsop leader, Chief Coboway – "Comowool," arrived at the fort on December 12, 1805, and was given a medal by Captain Lewis, who also presented the Chief with a list of the men in the Expedition. In March 1806, when the Corps of Discovery was ready to depart the Columbia, the Clatsops came to see them off. Chief Coboway was now given Fort Clatsop and its entire contents. Captain Lewis wrote admirably of the Chief, saying that he had been most kind and hospitable.

The British Northwest Company, the successor of John Jacob Astor's, Pacific Fur Company, was established at Fort Astoria, in 1814. On May 21, of that year, Chief Coboway visited Alexander Henry, and proudly showed him the expedition roster that Captain Lewis had given him.

In the journal of John Jewitt, it was noted by Captain Hill, of the American brig, *Lydia*, before he sailed for Canton, that he received a notice written by Lewis & Clark, which the captains left with the Indians on their departure from Fort Clatsop, and he mentioned that the Clatsop people had in their possession the medals that the explorers had given them.

A young Chinook woman saved the lives of the crew of the *Lydia* by forewarning them of a plan by her people to seize the ship.

The Indian tribes living near the river traded the pelts of the sea-otter, the beaver, fox and even elk. In return they received old muskets, copper kettles, blankets, red & blue cloth, sheet copper, brass, knives, tobacco, fishhooks, and buttons. The most favored items were the blue and white beads, which were on strands a fathom in length.

The traders who came to the great "river of the west" were noted by Clark:

> They arrive generally about the month of April, and either remain until October or return at that time; during which time, having no establishment on shore, they anchor on the north side of the bay, at the place already described, which is a spacious and commodious harbour.
>
> These strangers who visit the Columbia for the purpose of trade or hunting must be either English or Americans." Clark believed. "The Indians inform us that they speak the same language as we do…the greater part of them annually arrive in April, and either remain till autumn or revisit at that time which we could not clearly understand; the trade cannot be direct from either England or the United States, since the ships could not return thither during the remainder of the year. When the Indians are asked where these traders go on leaving the Columbia they always point to the southwest, whence we presume that they do not belong at any establishment at Nootka sound. They do, however, mention a trader by the name of Moore who sometimes touches at this place, and the last time he came he had on board three cows; and when he left them continued along the northwest coast, which renders it probable that there may be a settlement of whites in that direction. The names and description of all these persons who visit them in the spring and autumn are remembered with great accuracy, and we took down exactly as they were pronounced, the following list: The favourite trader is Mr. Haley, who visits them in a vessel with three masts, and continues some time.

Trading Vessels

The others are:

Youens, who comes also in a three-masted vessel, and is a trader.

Tallamon, in a three-masted vessel, but he is not a trader.

Callalamet, in a ship of the same size; he is a trader, and they say has a wooden leg.

Swipton – three masted vessel, trader.

Additional names of the traders were:

Mackey, Washington, Mesship, Davidson, Jackson, Bolch, and Skelley – also a trader, in a vessel with three masts; but he has been gone for some years. He had only one eye. (*History of the Expedition*, 1903, 152-153.)

Captain Hugh Moore of the British ship *Phoenix* from Bengal, was trading on the Northwest coast between 1792 and 1794. The Indians told Lewis & Clark that he had three cows on board. In Howay's "trading vessels" he calls her "our Mystery ship," like the *Jenny*, a record of her journey was never kept by the captain. She was the first vessel to spend the winter on the Columbia – the Hawaiian Islands was the preferred wintering location for the sea traders. Captain Broughton of the British navy met the *Jenny* on the Columbia in 1792. The other traders and their vessels that became known were:

Youens – Captain George Vancouver met a number of trading vessels in 1792, and one of these was the *Prince William Henry*, Ewen or Ewens the captain.

Tallamon – or Callamon, who was also trading with the Makah Indians near Cape Flattery.

Mackey – Magee, Captain James Magee of the American ship *Margaret* out of Boston, trading on the coast between 1792 and 1793. In 1802, he was trading on the river with the ship *Globe*. James Magee, James Lamb, Russell Sturgis and Stephen Hills were the owners of the *Sea Otter*.

Mesship – Winship, Captain Charles Winship, of the brigantine *Betsy* of Boston, trading on the coast in 1800, and Captain Jonathan Winship, one of the owners of the *O'Cain*, New York, trading between Alaska and California, 1803-1804.

Davidson – George Davidson from Boston for the Northwest coast in 1799, the commander of the schooner *Rover* built in Georgetown, and owned by the Dorr family of Boston. He had been with Captain Robert Gray, who successfully entered the river in 1792, and named the great river after his ship *Columbia*. He was an accomplished artist who painted various scenes of the river and the coast.

Bolch – Probably Captain William Bowles with the *Mary* out of Boston. She was in Canton in 1799, and trading on the coast 1802-1803. (Moulton, 2002, 155-156 and 159-161)

The *Caroline* under the command of Captain Derby was on the Columbia in 1802 and again in 1804, this we know, from a message cut into a tree near the entrance to the river: "Ship *Caroline* of Boston, May 21, 1804."

The *Sea Otter,* under Captain Hill of Boston, made the entrance to the Columbia in 1797, to begin trading with the Indians. Later that year she sailed for China to trade the collected pelts, valued at over $47,000. The successful enterprise sailed for home on January 8, 1798, with nearly "50,000 pounds of tea, 7,000 pieces of nankeens, 100 sets of china, 300 tea sets, and yards of silk fabric and thread. When the ship arrived in Boston on July 21, the customs duty paid was nearly equal to the value of the outbound cargo, the ship having made a profit of ten times the original investment." (Malloy, 1998, 106)

One of the most remarkable stories of survival by shipwrecked sailors, comes from the men of the *Sea Otter*. This English vessel was wrecked somewhere near the mouth of the Umpqua River, at Coos Bay, leaving four survivors of the lost ship: Baptiste Lavall, Michael Connors, Jean Lozier, and Emmanuel Silver. The four men owed their lives to the fact that they were hunting sea otters, on an island when the ferocious coastal storm hit, destroying the ship.

Trading Vessels

They crossed half of the country from the Pacific Ocean to Red River, Louisiana, by way of the Santiam Pass, through the Deschutes country, and finally to their destination at Red River, near Natchez on the Mississippi.

The tale of the overland journey was recalled in a letter from a man living in Natchez to a friend at Norfolk, printed in the "Louisiana Gazettte" for August 16, 1810. The story begins with Mr. Lavall, who was born in Philadelphia, and moved to Canada at the end of the Revolutionary War, where he was engaged in the fur trade. He became the heir to an estate, which required his travel to England, and from there he embarked on a trading voyage to the Northwest Coast:

> Your friend W – has overtaken me at this place, from whence we shall go in company to the Oppolusa country. As usual he is full of news, but what is most surprising he actually brings us something unusually interesting. He informs me that in descending the river, he fell in with a party of four men (or rather heroes) who after suffering shipwreck on the Northwest coast, had not only the spirit to plan but courage to attempt; and the fortitude to persevere and succeed on one of the most daring undertakings I have ever heard of, viz – journey across the continent from the Pacific to the Atlantic ocean, with no other provision than their guns with six pounds of powder and 20 pounds of shot. Incredible as this circumstance may appear, the short account given by Mr. Babtiste Lavall to Mr. W – carried the strongest evidence of the facts.
>
> Mr. Lavall was born in the city of Philadelphia, although a republican himself, yet the attachment of his father and family to the king rendered it necessary for them to remove to Canada after the close of the war, where he ever since has been engaged in the fur trade – That having fallen heir to an estate he went to England to receive it, and there embarked on a trading voyage to the North West Coast on board the schooner Sea Otter of 170 tons and commanded by John Niles – that he was part owner, as well as supercargo – and on the 22nd August 1808

the vessel, cargo and crew consisting of nine souls were all lost in a violent gale, about 200 miles south of the Columbia river; while he, together with Michael Conner, Jean Lozier, and Emmanuel Silver were providentially saved by being on a hunt on an uninhabited island – That after waiting some time, in hope of meeting with some vessel, they gave up that point in despair, when he prevailed on his companions to attempt to cross over the continent by land – That after passing through and endless number of strange and savage nations amongst whom they were often detained as prisoners, and suffering every privation and hardship that it was possible to endure they happily succeeded in accomplishing their desperate undertaking.

Winships

The Winship brothers — Abiel, Jonathan, and Nathan— arrived on the Columbia in 1810, with a company of thirty men, a year ahead of John Jacob Astor, aboard their sailing ship the *Albatross*, from Boston. They entered the river on May 26, and in early June selected a location, among some oak trees – Oak Point, for their settlement, a riverside location near present day Clatskanie and Rainier.

A fortress was built and gardens planted, but the flooding rains of early June soon covered their new home. A search for a new site, was conducted, but the Chinook Indians did not welcome the strangers to their country, discouraging the young family. So they boarded the *Albatross* on June 12, after loading the farm animals, they had brought ashore, and sailed down the river, never to return.

"Mouth of the Columbia River, from an original drawing."

"Mouth of the Columbia River, from an original drawing." Rev. C. G. Nicolay, of King's College, and Member of the Royal Geographical Society, London. 1846.

Astoria

A young redhead was first introduced to Americans at Fort Clatsop, when he visited the members of the Expedition. Sargeant Patrick Gass, made this entry in his journal for, November 23, 1805:

> In the afternoon ten of the Clatsop nation that live on the south side of the river came to our camp…One of these had the reddest hair I ever saw, and a fair skin, much freckled.

He returned on the last day of the year, the event recorded by Captain William Clark in his journal:

> Tuesday 31st December 1805 – "With the party of Clatsops who visited us last was a man of much lighter coloured than the natives are generally, he was freckled with long duskey red hair, about 25 years of age, and must certainly be half white at least,

this man appeared to understand more of the English language than the others of his party, but did not speak a word of English, he possessed all the habits of the Indians.

Alexander Henry recorded his adventures at Astoria in his "Manuscript Journals of a Fur Trader in the North-west Company," which were combined with those of the famous explorer and mapmaker, David Thompson, (David Thompson was the first explorer-surveyor to chart the entire length of the Columbia River, between 1807 and 1011.) to produce "New Light on the Early History of the Greater Northwest." On December 8th, 1813, he recorded the arrival of the Clatsop chief with a gift of salmon, and a most unusual young man:

> The old Clatsop chief arrived with some excellent salmon and the meat of a large biche. There came with him a man about 30 years of age, who had extraordinary dark red hair and is much freckled – a supposed offspring of a ship that was wrecked within a few miles of the entrance of this river many years ago. Great quantities of beeswax continue to be dug out of the sand near this spot, and the Indians bring it to trade with us.

In another entry he identifies the ship as Spanish, and again describes the beeswax as a trade article.

> Feb. 28th 1814: "They bring us frequently lumps of beeswax, fresh out of the sand, which they collect on the coast to the S., where the Spanish ship was cast away some years ago…"
>
> On Mar. 18th The Indians arrived with articles for trade and told him about wild cats they had seen in the woods, "and I suppose they may have originated from Spanish ships which have been cast away on this coast. We know of vessels having been lost only a few miles S. of the Columbia."
>
> On Dec. 14th he writes of their journey to investigate Fort Clatsop: "We walked up to see the old American winter quarters of Captains Lewis and Clark in 1805-06, which are in total ruins,

the wood having been cut down and destroyed by the Indians; but the remains are still visible. In the fort are already grown up shoots of willows 25 feet high."

On Jan. 7th "Comcomly came in with a long piece of bar iron…Comcomly traded two dressed otter-skins for a blanket and blue H. B. strouds. He took away a number of full and empty boxes, which he had deposited for safety when he moved from his village last summer. Some of these boxes are of Chinook manufacture, neatly made, and set round the sides and edges with sea shells…I saw in them a few copper coins of Russian money, about the size of a dollar;"

Apr. 8th "The old Clatsop chief, with some of his followers, brought a large beaver in meat, three trout, a few beaver skins, and a few pounds of beeswax. We reduced our price on Canton blue beads one-third;

The young redhead is described by both Henry and Clark as having dusky, or dark red hair, which helps to identify him, as well as the estimates of his age, 25 years old in 1805, at Fort Clatsop and then about 33 in 1813, at Fort Astoria.

One of the three clerks of Astor's company, Ross Cox, reports on the redhead, and states that he was the son of an English sailor:

An Indian belonging to a small tribe on the coast, to the southward of the Clatsops, occasionally visited the fort. He was a perfect 'lusus naturae' ("Lusus naturae" is defined by Webster's as a freak of nature) and his history was rather curious. His skin was fair, his face partially freckled, and his hair quite red. He was about five feet ten inches high, was slender, but remarkably well made; his head had not undergone the flattening process; and he was called *Jack Ramsay*, in consequence of that name having been punctured on his left arm. The Indians allege that his father was an English sailor, who had deserted from a trading vessel, and had lived many years among their tribe, one of whom he married; that when Jack was born, he insisted on preserving the child's head in its natural state, and while young had punctured the arm in the above manner. Old Ramsay had died about twenty years before this period; he had several more children, but Jack was the only red-headed one among them. He was the only half-bred I ever saw with red hair, as that race in general partake of the swarthy hue derived from their maternal ancestors. Poor Jack was fond of his father's country men, and had the decency to wear trousers whenever he came to the fort. We therefore made a collection of old clothes for his use, sufficient to last him for many years. (Cox, 1957, 170-171)

According to Ross Cox, Jack's father, "Old Ramsay" was an English sailor who deserted from a trading vessel and had lived many years with a tribe that was living to the south of the Clatsops, even taking a wife. To have a son of Jack's age, Ramsay must have left a ship that was visiting the Northwest coast about 1780, or earlier. It is possible that Ramsay jumped ship from one of the two vessels of the English expedition, under Captain Cook, 1778-1779, the *Discovery* and the *Resolution*, although Captain Cook reported no deserters.

Jack Tar jumped ship in Hawaii in 1811, in the dark of night, from the *Tonquin*, while it was anchored in Karakakooa bay, near the island, then known as "Owyhee" and within a mile of the site where Captain Cook died in 1779.

"Astoria in 1811." Fort Astoria by W. H. Gray. 1870.

Tonquin

The Pacific Fur Company ship, *Tonquin*, left New York harbor on September 6, 1810, under the command of Captain Jonathan Thorn, accompanied to the open sea, by "Old Ironsides" the *USS Constitution*. The *Tonquin* was bound for the Columbia River, with Astor's new company, to establish the first permanent settlement on the Pacific coast, with its first port-of-call at the Sandwich Islands – Hawaii. On board were the three company clerks, Gabriel Franchere, Alexander Ross and Ross Cox, who arrived at the mouth of the Columbia on March 22, 1811.

After the company members and their supplies were offloaded, the vessel proceeded north to Vancouver Island, on a trading mission from which it would never return. All three clerks at Astoria recorded the last days of the ship. One of the first reports of the ship's destruction to reach Fort Astoria, said that the Indian interpreter, Jack Ramsay, was the only survivor.

The ship left the Columbia on June 5, 1811, with Captain Thorn at the helm, accompanied by Alexander Mckay and James Lewis. Ross Cox said that "Mr M'Kay took on board, as an interpreter, a native of Gray's harbour, who was well aquainted with the various dialects of the tribes on the coast." After arriving at an anchorage in the Templar Channel at Clayoquot Sound, on the west coast of Vancouver Island, the crew began trading with the native people, against the advice of Ramsay, who warned the Captain of the dangers involved in trading with the Indians of this area. A number of Indian canoes came along side, bringing sea otter furs to trade and during the negotiations, Captain Thorn proved to be a rather impatient trader. After giving his price for the furs offered by Nookamis, the captain insulted the old chief, by rubbing a pelt in his face, and then dismissed him over the side.

The next morning the Indians appeared near the ship and indicated they were prepared to conduct business, by waving pelts over their heads. After climbing aboard they began trading for knives, to the alarm of the Captain, who now saw armed foreigners on the deck of his ship. Then a second canoe arrived and Thorn hurried to get McKay and Ramsay. They agreed the situation had become dangerous and urged the Captain to weigh anchor. He ordered all hands to the capstan, while other sailors scrambled aloft to unfurl the sails. At that moment, a great yell announced the attack by the Indians, who drew knives and hatchets hidden beneath their furs, killing Captain Thorn, Alexander McKay, and a number of crewmen. Ramsay jumped over the side and was rescued by some Indian women in a canoe. The invaders were driven off the ship by a number of survivors, who were able to break out firearms. Mr. Lewis was mortally wounded, but remained with his ship, while his companions escaped. The seamen rowed off in a small boat, but were captured after reaching shore, and were never seen again. The next day large numbers of natives took over the prized ship and began celebrating their victory, unaware of the presence of the only survivor, James Lewis, who set off the ship's powder magazine, completely destroying the *Tonquin* and all on board.

The earliest printed account of the fate of the ship appeared in the "Missouri Gazette" May 15, 1813, based on a report carried to St Louis by Robert Stuart. The 1854 edition of Gabriel Franchere's publication included the notation:

> It will never be known how or by whom the Tonquin was blown up. Some pretend to say that it was the work of James Lewis, but that is impossible, for it appears from the narrative of the Indian that he was one of the first persons murdered. It will be recollected that five men got between decks from aloft, during the affray, and only four were seen to quit the ship afterward in the boat. The presumption was that the missing man must have done it, and in further conversation with the Gray's harbor Indian, he inclined to that opinion, and even affirmed that the individual was the ship's armorer, Weeks. It might also have been accidental. There was a large quantity of powder in the run immediately under the cabin, and it is not impossible that while the Indians were intent on plunder, in opening some of the kegs they may have set a fire to the contents. Or again, the men, before quitting the ship, may have lighted a slow train, which is the most likely supposition of all.

At Fort Astoria, Gabriel Franchere wrote that "the Old Chief Concomly came to tell us that an Indian from Gray's harbor, who had sailed on the Tonquin in 1811, and who was the only one to escape the massacre of the crew of that ship, had returned to his tribe."

George Ramsay

This was not Jack Ramsay, however, but his brother, George Ramsay, who sailed aboard the *Tonquin* and escaped from the Indians, returning to Fort Astoria to report the destruction of the ship. The authors of "Indians of the Pacific Northwest" declared that George Ramsay was at Clayoquot Sound on the Vancouver Island shore when Captain Thorn had expelled the Indians from his ship. George endured a two-year enslavement in the north, until he was ransomed by friends. (Ruby and Brown, 1981, 31)

In addition to this new account, the writer Emma Gene Miller, related the details of an article by J. Neilson Barry, entitled, "Primary Sources of Early History of the Vicinity of Seaside, Oregon," which indicated that George Ramsay was known as Lamasay, and that Old Ramsay was a survivor of a shipwreck near Tillamook, about 1780. He married a native woman, and his son, who had red hair and a freckled face, was Jack Ramsay. When smallpox struck the native villages, he placed his family in safety and cared for those who were inflicted, but eventually he also succumbed to the plague.

Jack's brother, George Ramsay, was called Lamasay by the Chinook tribe. George was a pilot and an interpreter on ships, who spoke many Indian languages, including French and English, and was the only survivor from the *Tonquin*. (Miller, 1958, 18)

In the journal of Alfred Seton, the company clerk writes that George Ramsay was called "Lamasee" by the Indians, because they had such difficulty in pronouncing the letter "R." Seton's notebook was discovered in 1947, during renovation of Washington Irving's home in Tarrytown, New York, a most important source for Irving's "Astoria."

John C. Jackson in "Children of the Fur Trade" says Jack's brother George was taken aboard the *Tonquin* when the Americans of the Pacific Fur Co. were in Gray's harbor. Nootka visitors from Wickininish arrived at the fort with news of the loss of the ship. Men from the Northwest Co., the Hudson's Bay Co., and officers in the American Navy, knew George, also known as Qua-luk, as a reliable pilot. (Jackson, 1995, 7, and Barry, 1993, 297-301)

From the "Narrative of a Journey" by John Kirk Townsend, a member of Capt. Nathaniel Wyeth's expedition to the Oregon country, we follow along on the short voyage of the *May Dacre* down the Columbia, beginning on December 3, 1834:

"The navigation of the river is particularly difficult in consequence of numerous shoals and sand bars, and good pilots are scarce, the Indians alone officiating in that capacity. Towards noon the next day, a Kowalitsk Indian with but one eye, who said his name was George, boarded us, and showed a letter which he carried, written by Captain McNeall, in the Hudson's Bay service, recommending said George as a capable and experienced pilot. We accepted his service gladly, and made a bargain with him to take us into Baker's bay near the cape, for four bottles of rum; with the understanding, however, that every time the brig ran aground, one bottle of the precious liquor was to be forfeited. George agreed to the terms, and taking his station at the bow, gave orders to the man at the wheel like one having authority, pointing with his finger when he wished a deviation from the common course, and pronouncing in a loud voice the single word "ookook," (here)"

One of the ships on the United States Exploring Expedition, the *Peacock* was lost on the northern spit near the mouth of the Columbia, in 1839, and Old George guided the *Flying Fish*, another Expedition vessel, safely across the bar to aid the survivors of the *Peacock* at Baker's Bay. The leader of the Expedition, Lt. Charles Wilkes, sketched the Ramsay's in 1841.

George was also the pilot for the ship *Lausanne*, in May, 1840, captained by Josiah Spalding, and successfully guided the ship across the river entrance to anchor in Baker's Bay. Aboard the vessel was Jason Lee and 51 passengers of the Missionary Society of the Methodist Episcopal Church, from New York, via Hawaii, who offered articles of trade for beeswax from the Chinook Indians. Alexander Lattie guided the *Lausanne* as far as Pilot Rock and then Ramsay took over. The following day, the ship was met by another vessel bringing food and another pilot, known as George Washington, who completed the voyage to Fort Vancouver.

Solomon Smith and his wife Helen worked as missionaries among the Clatsop tribe, and their son Silas was personally acquainted with George Ramsey, and knew he was the interpreter on the Tonquin.

Historian J. Neilson Barry quotes from Silas Smith: "At Baker's Bay, an Indian by the name of Ramsay was engaged as river pilot, the same who was interpreter on the Tonquin at the time of her destruction at Clayoquot. He had only one eye, but was a good pilot, Ramsay was his English name." J. H. Frost speaks of George in 1840, and said a hair seal had scratched out his eye.

Finally, we learn that Jack Ramsay was seen again at Fort Vancouver The redhead's appearance was reported by John Keast Lord, in 1837, who believed that Jack was sixty years old. (Ruby and Brown, 1976, 261)

FORT GEORGE OR ASTORIA, COLUMBIA RIVER.—THE HUDSON'S BAY COMPANY'S ESTABLISHMENT.

Fort George. Fort Astoria became Fort George in 1813 under the British until 1818, when Astoria was returned to America. The drawing is from the "Illustrated London News" February 10, 1849.

Galleons and Junks
Tillamook

The name for the Indians, Killamook, is of Chinook origin and means the people of Nekelim or Nehalem country. Mrs. William Obrist, a full-blooded Tillamook and the granddaughter of Mrs. Ed Gervais, of Nehalem, said that in Tillamook pre-history only the Nehalem band of the Tillamook Indians were called the Killamooks. The tribe that lived on Tillamook Bay was known as the Hoquartons. The Great Kilamox Town, referred to by Lewis & Clark, was a favorite location for winter festivals where the Nehalems, the Tillamooks, and the Columbia River tribes gathered for festivities. A Nehalem village was also located at Wheeler, previously known by the pioneers, as Dean's Point.

The missionary journey of 1841, led by J. H. Frost, the first into Tillamook country, was "to procure some cattle and horses," and for butter and milk. The expedition party included Wakilkil, a Tillamook Indian guide, Lewis Taylor, an ex-sailor, and the famous Solomon Smith, with his horse, Machera, who carried the supplies.

The Tillamook Indians handed down the legend of a Spanish ship through Ilga Adams, who was also known as Old Adam. Lewis & Dryden's *Marine History of the Pacific Northwest*, from 1895, states that Adam's father had actually witnessed the wreck as a young man and said there were no survivors:

> In 1772, according to well-authenticated stories and traditions, one of Spain's Oriental fleet, while on a voyage from China, laden with beeswax and Chinese bric-a-brac, was blown to the northward and wrecked near the mouth of the Columbia. Most historical writers have given the location of this wreck as being on the Nehalem River, at which place large quantities of beeswax have been and are still being found. Aside from the presence of the beeswax and other traces of the wreck, the Tillamook Indians have had the story handed down with considerable ac-

curacy. Adam, a Tillamook chief, who died at Tillamook a few years ago, and who was a remarkably intelligent Indian, told the writer that his father, when a young man had witnessed the wreck, and that all of the crew were drowned. As Adam was over one hundred years old at the time of his death, there is no reason to doubt that the Nehalem beeswax ship, of which so much has been written was identical with the one wrecked on 1772." (Wright, 1895, 2 and Bancroft's appendix)

Ilga Adams was the hereditary chief of the Tillamooks, considered a sub-chief to Chief Kilchis. He was an expert hunter & trapper, and a skilled canoeman. He took many trips over the Tillamook bar up the coast to the trading post at Fort George. He met and married a Clatsop maiden, named Maggie, in her country, and returned home with his new bride, where they had four children. A priest from Grande Ronde arrived in the Tillamook country to baptize Ilga and his family, before he passed away in 1890.

Silas Smith

Solomon Howard Smith was a teacher at Fort Vancouver and French Prairie, a doctor, farmer, and a member of the early Oregon legislature. He came to Oregon with Nathaniel Wyeth in 1832, and in 1833, was teaching school at Fort Vancouver. There he met his wife, Helen, who was Celiast Coboway, one of the three daughters of Chief Coboway, of the Clatsops, who visited Lewis & Clark in 1805. He guided Daniel Lee to the mouth of the Columbia in May, 1840, to meet the *Lausanne* which was conveying the Great Reinforcement to Oregon. In August 1840, he drove a herd of cattle from Grande Ronde to Clatsop Plains, with the other famous missionary Joseph Frost. He took a donation land claim on the Clatsop Plains in the same year, and in 1841, purchased horses from Ewing Young, and herded them to the Plains from St Helens. He cared for the crew of the *Peacock* in 1841, and also the crew of the *Shark* in 1846. He practiced medicine, opened a dairy farm on the Plains and established the first Columbia River ferry. In 1849, he opened a general store at Skipanon, and then operated a sawmill on the Lewis & Clark River. He was elected the state senator for Columbia and Clatsop Counties in 1874; the last survivor of the first American settlers in Oregon.

One of the seven children of the Smith family, Silas B. Smith, was born in 1840. He began his education in Clatsop County and then left home to study at Dartmouth College, in Hanover, New Hampshire, under a scholarship offered to outstanding native Americans. After graduation, he studied law and began legal practice in Astoria.

On December 16, 1899, Silas delivered the first annual address of the Oregon Historical Society, which was later published in "Oregon Native Son," for January 1900:

> The first authenticated recorded account of the exploration of the Pacific Northwest coast by white men – not considering the mythical voyages of Lorenzo Ferer Maldonado, Juan de Fuca, and admiral Bartolome del Fonte, relating to their alleged discovery of the Straits of Anian – was that made by Lieutenant Juan Perez, of the Spanish navy, on the sloop of war Santiago, from San Blas, Mexico, in 1774, leaving that port on January 25, of that year on her northern cruise.
>
> Lieutenant Perez proceeded as far as the northernmost point of Queen Charlotte's island and doubling the point to the inland side turned south and returned to Monterey, Cal., mostly following the coast on the return voyage. But tradition among the Indian tribes at the mouth of the Columbia river and vicinity" relates that at least three vessels had visited their shores. "The treasure ship at Echanie mountain, the beeswax ship near the mouth of the Nehalem river and one other, just south of the mouth of the Columbia river.

Treasure Ship

> The treasure ship did not become a wreck; she dropped anchor as she approached land and sent a boat ashore with several men and a large chest or box. The box was taken up on

the southwest face of the mountain above the road and there buried. And some say that a man was then and there killed and buried with the chest. Then some characters were marked on a large stone which was placed on the spot of burial, and the men then returned to the vessel, when she again put to sea. The treasure character of the deposit is an inference of the whites and the alleged manner of entombment.

The natives have never pretended to know what was contained in the chest. The above is the substance of the account of the treasure ship at Ecahnie mountain as given by the older Indians in the early settlement of the country.

Beeswax Ship

Much has been told and written about the bees-wax wreck. It has gone into song and story. It has developed a sort of literature peculiarly its own, and the end is not yet.

The Indian account is something like this: That sometime ago, before the coming of the whites, a vessel was driven ashore in the vicinity of where the beeswax is now found, just north of the mouth of the Nehalem river.

The vessel became a wreck, but all or most of her crew survived. A large part of her cargo was this beeswax. The crew, unable to get away remained there with the natives several months, when by concerted action the Indians massacred the entire number, on account, as they claimed, that the whites disregarded their – the natives' – marital relations. The Indians also state in connection with the massacre, that the crew fought with slung-shots. It would appear from this that they had lost their arms and ammunition.

I think it not too hazardous to identify this wreck as the Spanish ship San Jose, which had left La Paz, Lower California, June 16, 1769, loaded with mission supplies for the Catholic mission at San Diego, Upper California, and of which nothing was ever heard after she left port. Every circumstance connected with the vessel and her journey favors this solution. Her course on her voyage was towards the north. Her mission supplies would include bees-wax or some other kind of wax as an article that would be needed for images, tapers, candles, etc. We find that some of the blocks of bees-wax from this wreck are inscribed with the Latin abbreviations "I.H.S." "Jesus Hominum Salvator," which abbreviation is, I believe, largely or commonly used in the Roman Catholic Church.

And we also find candles and tapers with the wicks in some, still remaining. And I believe a piece of this wax has now been found with the body of a bee imbedded in the wax.

This vessel falling in, in all probability, with a storm at sea while on her northward course, was driven away from her point of destination and found her fate on the sands at the mouth of the Nehalem River. The matter of the finding of the wax some 200 yards from the sea is accounted for by the fact that the crew, perhaps, endeavored to save the cargo, and carried part of it there, which afterwards became buried by the drifting sands.

The Treasure Committee of the Nehalem Valley Historical Society completed its findings in 1991, and published the results in "Tales of the Neahkahnie Treasure," which stated: "The San Jose sailing from San Blas, June 16, 1769, is believed by many historians to lie at the foot of Neahkahnie Mountain." (Jensen, 1990, 6)

Columbia Ship

The third vessel of which tradition speaks, and whose advent, I think, has priority of date to the others, came ashore about two miles south of the mouth of the Columbia River.

Two of the crew survived, one of whom was named Konapee. The orthography of this name is given here phonetically, as pronounced by the Indians. The vessel was cast far enough up on the beach as to be accessible at low tide. After being looted she was burned by the natives for her iron.

Konapee and his companion were taken prisoners and held as slaves. The former soon showed himself as a worker of iron, and could fashion knives and hatchets for his captors. The natives soon considered him too great a person to be held as a slave, and gave him and his friend their liberty. After their release they went up the river about a mile above the Indian village to a place now known as New Astoria, and there located their dwelling. After that the Indians called the place Konapee, and it was known by that name long after the country was being settled by the whites. These men always declared that their home was towards the rising sun. And after a year or two they started east up the Columbia river, but, after reaching the Cascades, they went no further and there intermarried with the natives.

"This wreck I believe to be a Spanish galleon. Gabriel Franchere tells in his "Narrative" that, on their first voyage up the Columbia river, in 1811, at an Indian dwelling not far below the Cascades, they found a blind old man – presumably blind from old age – who their guide said, was a white man, and that his name was Soto." Franchere was led by a Chinook Indian guide, named Coalpo, from the village of Wahkiakum.

Gabriel Franchere

The next day, the 8th, we did not proceed far before we encountered a very rapid current. Soon after, we saw a hut of Indians engaged in fishing, where we stopped to breakfast. We found here an old blind man, who gave us as cordial reception. Our guide said that he was a white man, and that his name was Soto. We learned from the mouth of the old man himself that he was the son of a Spaniard who had been wrecked at the mouth of the river; that a part of the crew on this occasion got safe ashore, but were all massacred by the Clatsops with the exception of four, who were spared and who married native women; that these four Spaniards, of whom his father was one, disgusted with the savage life, attempted to reach a settlement of their own nation toward the south, but had never been heard of since; and that when his father, with his companions, left the country, he himself was yet quite young.

Alfred Seton was employed as a clerk, like Franchere, and arrived at Astoria aboard the second company ship *Beaver* on May 9, 1812. In passing up river, Seton saw old blind Soto, and his cabin, describing him as a solitary fisherman.

My mother, Mrs. Helen Smith, used to tell that at Fort Vancouver, in the later 1820's she met a Cascades woman, who was reputed to be a descendent of Konapee; that she was already past middle life, and was much fairer in complexion than the other natives. This I would say, was Soto's daughter.

Silas said that the Indian name for the castaways was "tlon-hon-nipts" – "of those who drifted ashore." He also determined that the name of the survivor Konapee, may have been a corruption of the Spanish name "Juan de Pay". "The natives not being able to pronounce it according to the Spanish method, followed the sound as nearly as they could and called Juan, "Kon" de, "a" Pay, "pee." Silas believed that Soto would have been approximately 80 years old, when Gabriel Franchere met him in 1811, and placed the date of the shipwreck near the year 1725. (Smith, 1899, 443-446)

Soto

Lieutenant Broughton of the Vancouver expedition met Soto in 1792, and invited him aboard the *Chatham*. He accompanied the lieutenant on the survey of the river, and was highly regarded by the British commander, as "The friendly old chief."

Lewis & Clark visited his village on April 2, 1806: "All this time a very old blind man was speaking with great vehemence, apparently imploring his God."

On July 27, 1811, David Thompson ascending the river not far from Beacon Rock made this entry in his journal: "A canoe with a blind good old Chief came to us and smoked."

Three years later when Alexander Henry made a visit in 1814, he twice mentioned the Soto village, near Beacon Rock.

Soto had a daughter, according to J. Neilson Barry, who was much lighter than other natives, and his son was given a medal by Lewis & Clark. This medal is a treasured family heirloom, and is still held by the granddaughters of Chief Chenowith, Mrs. Mary V. Lane, and her sister Mrs. Isabel Underwood. The identification of the Lewis & Clark medal was made by Mr. Howland Wood, Curator of the American Numismatic Society. An illustration of the piece is shown in Swan's "The Northwest Coast." (Barry, 1932, 25-34. See also, Giesecke, Oregonian, 1959)

Smithsonian

The anthropologist, Franz Boas searched for Lower Chinook Indians during the summer of 1890 and 1891. He found only two people who spoke Chinook, living among the Chehalis on Willapa Bay. One was Charles Cultee, who supplied Mr. Boas with details for the Smithsonian Institution's study "Chinook Texts," published in 1894.

The "Chinook Texts" includes the story of the discovery of the shipwreck, near the entrance to the Columbia, by a Clatsop woman, which she described as a "monster," with "two bears" inside. The monster had "two trees standing" in it (masts) with "ropes tied to the trees." It was "shining" in the sun (a copper-sheathed bottom) and had many pieces of iron sticking into it. When additional members of the tribe followed the woman to the beach the two bears came out of the ship, with copper kettles in their hands, and indicated that they wanted the Indians to fetch water for them. Some of the natives climbed into the ship, seeing that it was like a very large canoe, full of boxes, and one man found a string of brass buttons. They burned the ship for the metal and took the two survivors as slaves.

Cullaby

In the "Legend of Nehalem," chapter 20 from Samuel Clarke's *Pioneer Days of Oregon History*, one reads of John Minto, the famous Salem author and state representative, and his visit with Cullaby in 1846. John Minto was born in Wylam, England in 1822, and began working in mines at the very young age of eight. He came to America in 1840 to work the Pennslvania mines and then left for Oregon, in 1844, to begin logging for Hunt's sawmill. In 1845, he purchased the Willamette Mission, and took a donation land claim in 1846, four miles south of Salem and began raising sheep. He became the secretary of the State Agricultural Society between 1867 and 1869, and helped organize the first Oregon Sate Fair. He became the editor of the "Willamette Farmer," in 1867 and was elected as state representative for three years, 1868-1870. He surveyed the Minto and Santiam Passes in 1882, and was the author of *Rhymes in Life in Oregon* and *Rhymes of Early Life in Oregon and Historical and Biographical Facts*. He was married to Martha Ann in 1847 and they had eight children.

> ...in 1846 – John Minto, then young and not long from England, who is well known in connection with pioneer history, at Cullaby's Lake met an Indian, who made his home there, and was descended from a white man who was saved from a wreck of prehistoric times...when asked concerning the red-headed Indian seen by Lewis and Clark, his answer was: 'Okook nica papa.' (That was my father)." (Clarke, 1905, 153)

John Minto was told the story of Cullaby by Edward Cullaby, his son. It is the account of a survivor of a ship, which was cast upon the shores near Tillamook. One survivor was discovered by Ona, a young Tillamook maiden, with a timber across his back. She cared for the castaway and erected a shelter near the place where he was found. He married Ona and taught her father how to use the new weapons from the shipwreck.

He became the gunsmith of the tribe, and joined them on hunting & fishing trips. The castaway proved to be a better spearsman than Ona's father, who was considered the expert in the tribe. He even saved the life of the chief's son, and a companion, who almost drowned, during a terrible storm. The chief's son became so jealous of the white man that he created conflict in the tribe. Ona's father and the young couple left the Tillamook village, to live with the Clatsops, and his sister was the wife of their chief. The new family made a home on the west shore of Cullaby Lake, and they also spent time at Neahcoxie, or at Quatat.

Sometime before 1800, a ship like the one he sailed on came near shore, in the home of the Tillamooks. Some of the crew came ashore leaving two men before departing. These two crewman soon died, spreading a disease through the Tillamooks and eventually to the Clatsops.

The survivor moved his family to a hunting camp near the Netul, now the Lewis & Clark River, to isolate them from the other infected members of the tribe. He then traveled to Quatat to aid the inflicted, where he also was stricken with the disease, which was probably smallpox, the "spotted death," and died soon after. (Miller, 1958, 18-21)

In *Legends and Traditions of Northwest History,* the Hon. Glenn N. Ranck writes that John Minto also saw there, at Morrison's – now Columbia Beach, approximately 8 miles south of Astoria, "a fair Indian girl so pale that he thought she was sick." He also stated that the girl was Cullaby's daughter. (Ranck, 1907, 37)

Cullaby's story was printed in the "Vacation News," a supplement to the Seaside Signal of September 16, 1955.

J. Neilson Barry received this account of Jack Ramsay's father direct from Mrs. Ellen Center, a granddaughter of Chief Kilchis, which was told to her by her father, who had learned this from his parents. A young sailor, with red hair, British or possibly Scottish, drifted into Nehalem Bay on a timber from a shipwreck about 1780. He was rescued by the Tillamook Indians, lived with them, married and had children. One of Jack Ramsay's daughters was married to Alexander Duncan Birnie, a famous guide, and the son of James Birnie, of the Hudson's Bay Company. (Barry, 1933, 297-298)

Nehalem Shore

Mr Warren said he had a piece of the "Beeswax ship of Nehalem" or it was "a piece of a junk which drifted across the Pacific... there were several sections" of a junk that drifted in near Nehalem, in 1893. The section was 20 feet long by 14 feet wide and six inches thick, assembled with "nails and dogs and also wooden pins" and caulked with tree bark.

Capt. F. S. Edwards, United States inspector of hulls, received the following interesting letter, the other day, from W. E. Warren, of Astoria, written at Elk Creek, concerning the famous beeswax ship remains of which have been found on the

Tillamook coast.

'I have a piece of the beeswax ship of Nehalem, which you are familiar with. I am almost certain it is a part of that vessel, if there ever was a vessel wrecked there in early days. This packet, or whatever it was, must have been built at least 200 years ago, or it is a piece of junk which drifted across the pacific. As I am not familiar with the construction of junks, I thought you might find someone who was. There were several sections of the junk washed in, two years ago, but they were at a place where it was worth a man's life to go. I saw them while fishing one day, and then I found one piece close to my place, on the sand where I can get close to it with a team. The piece I refer to is about 20 feet long, 14 feet wide and six inches thick. The boat was put together with nails and dogs and also wooden pins. She was caulked with the bark of a tree. Altogether, the craft must have been a peculiar one.'

Capt. Edwards will go to Astoria and secure a piece of the boat, if he can, for the collection in the inspector's office. (*Tillamook Headlight* – August 29, 1895, "The Beeswax Ship.")

'In the *Oregonian,* the following communication from Mr. Geo. W. Snell, of Snell, Heitshu & Woodard, seems to prove conclusively that the material found on the Nehalem coast which has time and again caused fruitless discussion, is not mineral wax, but pure beeswax.' He says:

While not a matter of public interest probably, last confirm-ing Messrs A. W. Miller's and Fullerton's opinion and belief that the substance found at Tillamook is beeswax, pure and simple. Hodge, Caief & Co. many years since purchased some three quarters of a ton of that article, putting in marketable shape with no question as to its identity, shipping the same to New York city, where it had ready sale, as pure beeswax, as it did in this market, for all purposes for which it is used; the heat is melting, notwithstanding the unknown years of exposure on the beach, developing the honey color very noticeably, while in appearance, after remolding, it was superior to later productions. The crude letters and figures referred to by Mr. Miller, were very plain on many pieces.

In 1894, a raging storm on the Oregon coast sent part of a shipwreck floating to Arch Cape, where it was located and later taken to the *Astoria Daily Budget*. The newspaper printed a sketch of this piece of ship wreckage, for the issue of April 21, 1894. The planks found in the sands by Mr. Warren, that were 20 feet long, with dowell pins and Iron clamps, sounds a great deal like this piece of ship wreckage.

The following narrative is by Samuel A. Clarke in "Wrecked Beeswax and Buried Treasure," *Oregon Native Son*, September, 1899:

> Great interest has been taken in Oregon concerning pre-historic wrecks that occurred long before occupancy by the whites. The chief testimony as to them comes from aboriginal sources, and is sometimes lost in the mists of the primitive era. Pieces of obsolete wreckage have been resurrected from the sands, and abundant evidence is found in masses of beeswax, that is indestructible, also found on the ocean shore south of the Columbia.

> Beeswax is not given to romance, save, perhaps, when taking shape in Mrs. Jarley's wax works, for commercial beeswax is one of the most unsentimental articles of commerce. The original comb that holds the luscious stores of the preternaturally 'busy bee' may touch on the romantic, or, as a taper used to illume festive scenes before coal gas or fragrant kerosene and the electric lights of today became illuminators, might have been a theme to treat of; but the beeswax of Nehalem, pounded in the surf until battered and blackened out of all recognition, had no essential claim for inspiration until its history developed to cause imagination and fancy to wonder at its origin.

> When Lewis and Clark wintered at the mouth of the Columbia – not quite a century ago – they learned the first we knew

officially of this flotsam of the seas, for they told of seeing it in the hands of natives. In 1814, one Henry, connected with the fur trade, who traveled and wrote of what he saw, published to the British world that beeswax had been dug out of the sands and was found drifting on the ocean shore, to his great wonder. It is thus evident that the memory of living man goes back to the time when this beeswax was not known to the natives at the mouth of the great river.

My personal cognizance of it goes back to 1870, when my family made a summer trip from the Willamette to Tillamook, 50 or 60 miles south of the Columbia, and brought back small pieces of the beeswax, and also various traditions concerning the ancient wrecks that might have left it there. The bones of two wrecks were then to be seen at the mouth of the Nehalem river, that enters the ocean a few miles north of Tillamook bay.

The Indians then occupied their ancient fishing grounds and hunted in the Coast range adjoining. Their story of historic wrecks varied. The sands of Nehalem seem to have rivaled and Charybdis in enticement to danger, for they rehearsed the story of a Chinese junk that met it fate on one side of the entrance, from which a number were saved. These lamented their fate and wept bitter tears as they looked over the sunset seas toward the shores of the Orient, where the waves were chanting the anthem of the 'Nevermore,' as friends unavailingly awaited their homecoming. But in time they made homes and found wives, leaving descendants whose almond eyes tell of their Oriental origin to this day.

Many supposed that this beeswax, afloat and ashore, had been a Chinese product, and as time had broken up the frame of the vessel it had washed ashore. To give wider field for specula-tion, occasionally wax candles and tapers were discovered, but the pundits explained that the Chinese had use for wax tapers in the worship of Joss.

When placing a specimen of this wax in the hands of Profes-sor Henry, of the Smithsonian, in 1872, this same legend accom-panied it. But, as time passed the stores of wax have increased. A fortunate ferryman who plays Charon on the Nehalem, found stores of this same wax on his own land claim, above all ocean tides, and an hundred yards or so distant from the beach. Here was a riddle worth unraveling.

This same beeswax has been found in blocks two feet by 16 inches in size and four inches thick, and these blocks, it has been said by scientific men, bear cabalistic characters that no man can understand, though skillful artists have copied them. Thus the mystery grew; and what made it even more mysterious, tradition did not limit Neptune's wreckage to that poor Chinaman, but told of other vessels lost her, no doubt belonging to western nations, as the men found dead on the sands were bronzed and bearded, as were the few who came ashore and tried to reach civilization by an overland route.

If this story of a white man's ship has any truth, then the beeswax story has greater room to bourgeon and breadth to grow. Determined to investigate, several years ago I went to Astoria and there met Mr. W. E. Warren, who proved to be a good witness. He had in his possession a block of this beeswax that his father received 26 years ago from the master of a schooner he then owned, that made trips out of the Columbia to near points along the coast, He has secured this great block of wax and brought it to his owner, whose son had kept it all this time as a message from the seas worth retaining until some solution might be had for the amazing story.

Though somewhat broken, this block was about the size alluded to, and must have weighed 20 pounds. On its upper face was a perfect capital 'N' cut wide and deep, at least five inches long, in exact shape of a Roman letter of this day. Over the 'N' was a diamond cut of proportionate size.

Since returning from Astoria I have seen in possession of Mr. Adolph Dekum another block, also broken, with these same marks, also part of a capital, figure 9, same size; the block having broken off through this figure. Mr. Dekum also has the lower part of a great taper 2.5 inches at the base, 10 inches of length remaining; the top has been broken off. The wick in this is not all gone; usually the wicks have rotted and there is a cavity where the wick once was. He also has a 10-inch piece of a small taper.

Mr. Warren is much interested in all that is prehistoric, as well as in early history. He took me to Mr. Thomas Linville, who also had a large block of same shape, much broken, with the letters 'I H' very plain and large size. Close to the last letter the block was broken off; he said there was another letter on the other piece. He had given this to a friend and went to get it to put the whole together, but his friend had sent it as a curiosity to his people in Philadelphia; he remembered that it had the letter 'N' on it and in the upper corner was a little 'S' with a stroke like a dollar mark. The whole block had been marked 'I H N,' with the small 's' and the stroke through it.

Mr. Linville tells a very interesting story. Both he and Mr. Warren have been on the ground and seen how the wax was stored and found. In 1885, seeking rest and health, Mr. Linville went to Nehalem beach and spent a month, stopping with a Mr. Howell, who kept a ferry across the Nehalem. No wagon travel was possible along that mountain shore, but he ferried over footmen, horsemen and livestock. He has lived there about 15 years. The wax was discovered before that, but since his time something near 10,000 pounds had been found and marketed at 20 cents per pound.

The Nehalem courses down from the Coast ranges, touches the base of Necarney, then turns south for three miles, parallel with and quite near to the ocean, then is lost in the sea. It is all this distance separated from the sea by only a narrow ridge, that no doubt has been thrown up as sea beaches. At the base of Necarney there is a small bay; along the ridge trees grow, among which the Nehalems built a village and made it their winter home.

The Indians have legends of several wrecks, that occurred in the olden time. The identity of the one that had the beeswax is the important question. So long as only indistinct marks were found it was imagined that the Chinese junk would do; but as soon as other markings were discovered, then I knew that the

Chinaman was not an interested party.

Mr. Howell's story was, that seven years before 1895, there was a very high wind without rain, that blew away the loose sand on the ridge 300 yards from his ferry; that he saw something left exposed and found it to be the corner of a block of beeswax. He dug it out and found a large block, the same as had been washed on the shore by the tides. He dug and found more; kept digging and found several tons of it in all shapes, sorts and sizes. Some has been run into boxes or kegs; a part was in the great squares or parallelograms. A number were marked with large capitals 'I H S' with a cross, evidently standing for 'In hoc signo' (in this sign). Others had the letters 'I. H. N.' for the Latin, 'In hoc nomen' (in this name). Some had only the letter 'N,' surmounted with a diamond. This, with the perfect tapers of different sizes, place it beyond doubt that the beeswax was intended for stores of the Catholic missions that were on the coast a hundred and fifty years ago.

The most perfect block of all was sold to Mr. Marshall J. Kinney, the well-known canneryman, in the salmon trade. It was most unfortunately burned when his factory was destroyed by fire some years ago. A very interesting question arises as to when this wreck occurred. How this ship came on this shore so long ago? And what use any mission, or any class of missions, could have had for so enormous a quantity of beeswax?

A very clear story, of Indian descent, traces an Indian family to a red-haired white man saved from a wreck about the year 1745. The traditions of wrecks say they occurred very long ago. The presence of that quantity of beeswax, found in a sandbank that is at least 10 feet above the highest tides and 100 paces from the present shore, challenges the records of time as to how long it may have been since this beach has risen out of the sea, and so locate the era when this wreck could have occurred. It is well known that this western coast is gradually rising from the sea, but that it could rise 15 or more feet before the cargo buried in the sands should be unearthed, must have required a term that spanned more than a century.

Another version of this beeswax wreck was given me by John Henry Brown, who said he received it from Captain Hobson, long known at Astoria as a bar pilot, who narrated it to a group of pioneers assembled for the annual meeting at Portland, in 1895. He had made visits to the Nehalem country, and on one of these excursions met one of the very first settlers, who said that many years ago the oldest of the Indians told a tradition handed down of a vessel lost very long ago; that all on board were lost and the vessel went gradually to decay; then the beeswax began to come ashore. They did not know what use to put it to; some tried burning it and found it was good fuel, but wood was plenty, so it was to valuable. They had an idea it might be bad medicine; at any rate, they quit burning it. This is the only tradition coming from Indian sources. Since 1806 white men have known of the Nehalem beeswax; geologists tell that the west coast is rising from the sea; that the Willamette valley was once a sound, as Puget sound is today; this wax was spread along the coast for 50 or more miles; therefore, it is not unreasonable to believe that the total quantity at the beginning was far more than we have knowledge of. But the most interesting question is: How came any such mission craft to be in this latitude a century and a half ago?

Long before Sir Walter Raleigh settled Virginia, or the Puritans landed in New England, Spaniards were sailing up the Pacific. The course of Spain's commerce was by the northern route, but what such a vessel was sent there in the middle of the last century is a question not easily answered. In that early day there were English, Dutch and other depredating on Spain's commerce, capturing treasure ships from Panama to China, as well as ships loaded with silks and spices from the Orient, bound to Panama, where these cargoes were taken by portage to the shore of the Atlantic and shipped for Spain. It is possible that some of these sea rovers had captured this mission ship and left the beeswax in her hold, and when the vessel was wrecked the same came ashore as we have found.

The story of old-time wrecks on the west shore has not

been yet told. I have gathered from reliable sources what could be known as to these, and will try to write concerning them at some near time." (Clarke, *Oregon Native Son*, 1899.)

James Wickersham

Burford Wilkinson described two Chinese coins which adorned the neck of a Clatsop woman, he met in 1900. The coins were also known as "Konapee's money" mentioned by the marine historian James Gibbs in "Oregon's Salty Coast." He lived near the south entrance of the Columbia near present-day Hammond, which became known as Konapee, and carried a great number of Chinese coins with him when he came ashore. (Gibbs, 1978, 29)

The Chinese coins had "a small, square hole in the center of the piece. The natives preserved these and used them as ornaments on their wampums and other ways, and had them even in my day," Silas Smith recalls, "and would always call them Konapee's money. I have some of these coins here which my mother had obtained from the Indians some 40 or 50 years ago." (Becham, 2006, 16)

Chinese coins were purchased by Judge James Wickersham from the Clatsops, that were dated to the reign of Chien Lung, 1736-1796, and the coins were collected from the shipwreck by the Clatsops, near their village. Mr. Wickersham speaks of the Clatsop history in his article for the *Oregon Native Son*, concerning the early wrecks on the Oregon coast.

James Wickersham:

"The 'beeswax wreck' at Nehalem beach, Oregon, has long interested thoughtful inquirers, who have generally attributed it to Chinese or Japanese sources. Sir Edward Belcher visited the Columbia River in 1839, and in his "Voyage Around the World" says of this wreck:

A wreck likewise occurred in this bay many years ago – It appears that a vessel, with many hands on board, and laden with beeswax, entered the bay and was wrecked; she went to pieces and the crew got on shore. Many articles were washed on shore, and particularly the beeswax. The latter is even now occasionally thrown upon the beach, but in smaller quantities than formerly. I have one specimen now in my possession.

In the *Pacific Coast Pilot*, 1889, Prof. George Davidson speaks of this wreck as a "Chinese or Japanese junk," and says that much beeswax is yet thrown ashore, specimens of which he secured. Horace Davis and Charles Wolcott Brooks in their interesting monographs of Japanese wrecks along the North Pacific coast, refer to this wreck, as do many other authors, but no one has presented such valuable and interesting facts about it as Mr. Samuel A. Clarke, in the Oregon Native Son for September, 1899.

Mr. Clarke describes the marks on these beeswax cakes saying:

> A number were marked with large capitals, 'I.H.S.' with a cross, evidently standing for 'In hoc signo' (in this sign). Others had the letters 'I.H.N.,' for the Latin, "In hoc nomen' (in this name). Some had only the letter 'N' surmounted with a diamond. This, with the perfect tapers of different sizes, placed it beyond doubt that the beeswax was intended for stores of the Catholic missions that were on the coast a hundred and fifty years ago.

If we may accept these statements as correct, they fairly settle the question of the origin of the 'beeswax wreck' of Nehalem. Many Japanese wrecks have been cast upon these coasts in times past and some may have carried beeswax, but there is only the slightest possibility that the cargo would have been marked with such characters as Mr. Clarke finds on the Nehalem beeswax. Granting the correctness of his rendering of the marks on the cargo, there is but little trouble to fairly answer his inquiry: How came such mission craft to be in this latitude a century and a half ago?

To begin with, its presence at Nehalem must have been accidental, for there were no missions north of San Francisco until long after this wreck was known. The small and widely separated missions among the natives of California had no need of such a great cargo of supplies, and it could only have been intended for the Church of Mexico.

A century and a half ago Spain yet carried on the trade with the Philippines from Manila to Acapulco by the northern route, striking the California coast in the latitude of Cape Mendocino and coasting southward to the Mexican port.

In 1595 the governor of the Philippines ordered Sebastian Rodriquez Cermennon, captain of the galleon San Augustin, to carefully inspect this northern route on his voyage from Manila to Acapulco, and if possible to locate a safe harbor for the annual eastern-bound galleons on the outer coast of California. In attempting to perform this service the San Augustin was wrecked at the old La Puerto de San Francisco, which was then unknown. The Spanish viceroy in Mexico sent out Vizcaino, in 1602, to survey these upper coasts, and incidentally to find the San Augustin, and from *Venegas' History of California*, 1757, a portion of Vizcaino's log-book is quoted:

> The San Augustin…was driven ashore in this harbor by the violence of the wind…and they had left ashore great quantities of wax and several chests of silk; and the general was desirous of putting in here to see if there remained any vestige of the ship and cargo.

Vizcaino found neither the wrecked vessel nor its cargo of wax at La Puerto de San Francisco in 1603; it had evidently floated at some storm or high tide and appears no more in the history of the coast. The Indian traditions at Nehalem recount how, long ago, the beeswax wreck came ashore, and all persons on board were lost; others maintain that part of the crew came ashore, and while some remained among the Indians, others went overland to their own people. Mr. Howell, the ferryman at Nehalem, found several tons of wax on his land high above the ocean tides, and a hundred yards distance from the beach. This mass of the cargo may have been gathered by the Indians, or by the crew of the San Augustin…and why not Nehalem? Could it be possible that a mistake was made and that the San Augustin was wrecked at Nehalem instead of La Puerto de San Francisco?

Certain facts may be accepted as established in this inquiry, viz: the Nehalem wax bears marks that clearly point to its use only by the Catholic Church; its presence in the Nehalem sands is accidental, without doubt; no such stores were needed or used north of Acapulco; the old San Augustin was loaded with that character of cargo intended for the Church in Mexico; no other such cargo is known to have been lost on the coast of California; and it is a reasonable, though not certain, conclusion that the old San Augustin, with her cargo of wax, and possibly a part of her crew, was cast away upon the Nehalem beach after disappearing from behind Point Reyes. It is said that remains of the old wreck have been seen at Nehalem, and it is hoped that Mr. Clarke, or some other equally competent observer, will give it a careful examination that it may be determined what manner of vessel the old 'beeswax wreck' was.

Was the beeswax wreck a 'Chinese or Japanese junk?

That a Japanese wreck came ashore at the Clatsop beach, a few miles north of the Nehalem, is beyond question, and Prof. Davidson, in the *Pacific Coast Pilot* of 1889, says this vessel was loaded with beeswax. I think he is mistaken in this statement. It is well known that the drift of the inshore current from Nehalem is northward; and Mr. Clarke points out that the beeswax is scattered fifty miles along the coast, or up to the Clatsop beach. Without a source of supplies, for the Clatsop wax can be surely located there, it is reasonable to conclude that it all came from the Nehalem quarry. Still there can be no doubt about the truth of the Indian tradition of a Japanese wreck at the Clatsop, although Mr. Clarke locates one which he calls Chinese at Nehalem.

Last summer I visited the Indians living at Sholwater Bay, just north of the Columbia river. Here, at the Bay Center Indian town, lives old 'Cheesht,' a Clatsop woman who was born at the Clatsop village some sixty or seventy years ago. She gave me the story of the Clatsop wreck, and exhibited an old 'hiqua' shell ornament, fringed at the bottom with Chinese coins. She said that many years ago – when her great-great grand-mother was a girl – that a wreck came ashore, and five men landed alive at the Clatsop village. One of these men married her great-great grand-mother, from whom these coins descended, having remained always in her family. The wrecked crew remained for a long time with the Clatsops, when some of them went up the Columbia river and never came back. Old Cheesht knew of the Nehalem wreck, and stated that they were entirely separate incidents. I purchased the old vestment with its Chinese coin fringe, and submitted the coins to a Chinese scholar, who found that each of them bore the characters of an Emperor who reigned from 1736 to 1799. It would seem, then, that this wreck could not have occurred earlier than 1736 – indeed, from her carefully-stated family chronology I concluded that it occurred about 1750. Some time afterwards I found a string of old Chinese coins among the Cowlitz Indians, and careful inquiry revealed that they had been heirlooms in old families long before the white men came. They dated from 1614 to 1796, and after careful inquiry I became convinced that they were a portion of the coins off the Clatsop wreck, having possibly been carried up the Columbia by the wrecked sailors, or received in trade from the Clatsop people, with whom the Cowlitz traded and intermarried.

Japanese wrecks have been cast away on the Pacific coast ever since our acquaintance with the region, and it is a familiar theory that much of the pre-Columbia civilization of America came over the 'black stream' from the land of the Rising Sun. However, it appears that the Nehalem wreck was Spanish, and not to be confounded with the Japanese wreck at Clatsop. It is at least probable that the Nehalem wreck was the second casting away of the Manila galleon San Augustin of 1595." (Wickersham, *Oregon Native Son*, vol. 1, May 1899 – April 1900, "Pre-Historic North Pacific Wrecks" 540-542.)

Notes:

Cheesht, the Clatsop Indian woman, wore the "hiqua shell ornament, with the Chinese coins" inherited from her great-great grandmother. Judge Wickersham purchased this necklace. The coins were from the reign of the emperor, Ching Lung 1736-1796.

In addition to the Clatsop wreck, ca. 1750, she also knew of the shipwreck at Nehalem.

When Vizcaino arrived at Drake's Bay, the *San Agustin* was not to be found.

The beeswax inscriptions indicate a Spanish cargo. Professor Davidson says the Japanese wreck on Clatsop beach was loaded with beeswax.

About the Author:

James Wickersham was born in Illinois, in 1857, and moved to the Washington Territory with his wife, Deborah, in 1883. He was a judge in Tacoma and was elected to the House of Representatives, in 1898. In 1900, he was appointed a District Judge by President McKinley, first judge of Alaska's interior. He covered his circuit by dogsled in winter and by boat in summer, but also found time to enjoy the magnificent last great wilderness. While hunting and hiking in the mountains of Alaska, he visited native villages, learning their history, and in 1903 he led the first attempt to climb Mt. McKinley. In 1908, he was elected to Alaska's Congress, and in 1916 he introduced the first Statehood Bill. He helped create the early Alaska Agricultural College that later became the University of Alaska.

Samuel A. Clarke

It is a fact that ancient coins have been found among the Indians, and Mr. Minto told me that he saw in the hands of an Indian there, so far back as the forties, a spear-head that was of elaborate work, with pike and axe as well as the spear. This weapon was of copper and beautifully inlaid, as no ordinary man would have.

T. A. Wood, author of *Beauty, Beeswax and Rum*, recalled how he had obtained from the Tillamook burial grounds, a Spanish coin of the 16th century and saw images of a stone cross and a figure representing the Savior.

Mr. W. E. Warren, of Astoria, has planks found in the sand, so deeply buried as to be perfectly preserved, that must have come from some wreck. One is 18 feet long, 2 feet wide and 5 inches through, bolted with dowell pins, clamped with six inch iron clamps – clamps 6 inches long, one and a half inch wide, and a half inch thick. He found very old-fashioned iron nails, flat, and heads turned down, 10 inches long and one and a half inch wide.

Capt. Kohner, uncle to Mr. W. E. Warren, got the block, (beeswax) he now has in 1870, and brought it to Warren's father. Before the discovery of the Columbia the Indians used to meet trading vessels that came outside and fired guns to notify them to bring their furs and skins to them to trade. These traders were white men and wore beards, but used Chinese cash to trade with; copper money that had square holes in them.

About 1825, soon after removing to Vancouver, word came that a Japanese junk was wrecked south of Cape Flattery. When he heard it Dr. McLoughlin sent there for the wrecked mariners and sent them to London to be forwarded to Japan. This was probably the vessel that had porcelain ware on board, that was scattered along the beach after the wreck. Some of this was saved in good order and brought over to Vancouver. I had this story from Dr. William McKay, who was brought up in Dr. McLoughlin's family."

Mr. Warren's mother heard the tale of the shipwreck at Necarney Bay from Swan, a very old Clatsop, who was told the story by his father when he was quite young; the story of some strange men who came ashore and buried a chest somewhere on Neahkahnie Mountain.

Note:

"Porcelain ware" from the Japanese wreck was determined to be in "good condition" and taken to Fort Vancouver. (Related by Dr. William McKay.)

J. Q. A. Bowlby

Mr. Bowlby, writing in 1900, believed that the ship wreckage with cannons that drifted to present day Cannon Beach, was from the *Peacock*.

I have read the article of S. A. Clarke in the September number of the Oregon Native Son, on Nehalem bees-wax. I have also seen the 'Warren' and 'Lindville' pieces of wax referred to by Mr. S. A. Clarke and agree with him that the characters on the Warren block are a capital letter 'N' with a diamond over it.

I am not able to make out a letter 'H' on the Lindville block, and the 'S' is doubtful. The latter block was on exhibition at the Exposition at Chicago, after which it was returned to the rooms of Messrs. Harris & Wright, in Astoria, where I saw it before the characters were removed. A portion of the block is still here, but all the characters, have been cut off. When I saw it first, I drew as accurately as I could without measurements the characters on its face.

The first on the top line may be an 'I' and the next an 'N,' but the third and last has very little resemblance to an 'S.' The two characters in the lower line do not seem to resemble any letter, although the second might be thought to resemble an inverted L. Recently I showed my draft of these characters to Mr. Lindville and he says they are correct, according to his memory, and represent all the characters he ever saw on the block.

There is another block of wax in Astoria. It is about nine by thirteen inches, and four inches thick. It is now in the possession of the family of Mr. N. Clinton, and was received from the family of Capt. Crosby, deceased. The characters are in the shape of a monogram, and are called by some a 'dollar-mark' and by others 'I.H.S.' The 'I' is placed upon the center of the 'S' and the 'H' is placed horizontally across the top of them.

The photograph of it shows the 'H' quite plainly, but the wax does not disclose the upper line of the 'H' so well.

It creates some doubt in my mind as to having been made by any person. The face of the wax has been shaved and worn off considerably, while there are cracks and niches in the wax that seem to have been made my shrinking or by wear during the long exposure.

I enclose photographs of the Warren and Clinton wax taken by Dr. Tuttle of this city. The doctor once saw a block with three numerals upon it; he thinks 'I' and '7' were two of them, but does not remember what the third one was. Much of the Nehalem wax was melted, molded and delivered to Foard & Stokes of this city as merchandise. In the Oregonian a year or two ago were printed several characters found on Nehalem wax.

W. E. Warren and Mark Warren found large pieces of wreckage near Cannon Beach, north of Nehalem, a few years since, but cut most of it into firewood. Capt. Edwards, of Portland, may have a portion. The timbers seem to have been fastened together differently from the manner of the present day. The nails were hand made and every iron fastening was trunneled with wood. Some of the timber resembled the wood in tea boxes.

Some portions of the Peacock, wrecked at the mouth of the Columbia river, went ashore at this place, however, and the wreckage found by the Warrens may have been a portion of that vessel. The Peacock wreckage carried two guns to the shore, hence the name of Cannon Beach, and one of the guns is there in charge of Mrs. Austin.

John Hobson

As I was coming to the Pioneer Reunion at Portland I bought a large piece of beeswax, not mineral wax, as some would like to have it, with the letters 'I.H.S.' on its face, which I know was on it when taken from the sand, at the mouth of the Nehalem river in 1868, by a man named Baker, from whom I purchased it the same year I brought it to Astoria, where it has remained ever since. I sold it to Captain Alfred Crosby, and after his death, and the removal of the family one of his sons presented it to Mr. Nicolas Clinton, who is the present owner. Any one wishing to see it, may do so by calling at his residence at Astoria. I have seen many articles, written about this wax, and many theories advanced in regard to how it got there. From nearly all I differ.

When I first came here, 51 years ago, there was beeswax among the Indians, from the Salmon river on the south to the Columbia on the north. They did not know what it was, using it for lights and leaky canvas. They said it came from a wreck, near the mouth of Nehalem river. The peninsula between the ocean and Nehalem, is about one and a half miles north and south, and half a mile east and west, and about two or three feet above ordinary high tides, and is an uneven flat of small sand dunes. This is where the wax has been found.

In talking with the Indians from that place often, they would tell us of the wreck, and of the vessel that brought the gold and silver coin, and carried it up Necarney mountain, and would refer us to some very old Indians, who ever came to Clatsop. After the wreck of the Hudson's Bay Company's bark "Vancouver," in 1848, a large case of drugs came on shore, near that place. Solomon H. Smith, and myself, concluded we would go down and buy the drugs and find out what we could from the old Indians about the wax and money vessels…We thought the wax vessel must have been a Chinese junk as we had seen several pieces of a junk between Clatsop and Nehalem.

After the Nehalem country became settled by the whites, and coal was discovered, a corps of government engineers was sent from the surveying schooner, lying at Astoria, to survey the Nehalem river, and bar. I, being acquainted with the country and routes, was hired, with horses, to take them down, and bring them back when they had finished the work. This was in 1868. This peninsula lies on the line of travel of all the coast, and the wax was scattered all over it, and the constant winds blowing the sands from the northwest in summer and the southwest in winter, has covered and uncovered it for ages, and the sun has softened it into different shapes and sizes. Some pieces were bleached nearly white. There was much dirt and sand in it, which stuck to it when softened by the sun. Here is where the Indians used to pick it up, when crossing this waste. When the whites came here to settle they collected wax, and one, Baker, made a business of it, and found that the most of it when exposed to view, was lying on a thin stratum of earth, like the sediment of a river freshet (which I believe it was), and scattered all over the peninsula. Baker took his spade and would prospect the sand dunes. If the clay stratum was found, he would follow it up, and find large quantities of wax in all conceivable shapes and sizes, including many candles from one and a half inches to two inches in diameter, and where the sun had closed the end the wicks were perfect. Judge McGuire, of Seaside, has some of the candles. I believe that some time after the wreck there was a very high freshet in the river, which spread the wax, logs and timbers all over the peninsula.

One of these dunes, many of them, logs rotted and grass grew in places and the drifting sands would sweep over them, thus protecting the wax, and the stratum, for there were remnants of rotten wood in most of them. The one in which this large piece was found, was near the center of the spit. There was also found the remnant of a ship timber, with some rusty, wrought iron nails, four square, thin at head, even taper from head to point, about six or eight inches long, and about five-eights of an inch thick at the head. There was also a copper chain, about 50 inches long, with a swivel in the middle of it; links four or five inches long, and five-eighth-wire. It was brought from that place by J. Larsen, and changed ownership several times, being finally placed in the mining bureau in San Francisco by Mr. Charles Hughes.

I do not pretend to know where these remnants came from, but believe the vessel to have been English, or Spanish, from China, freighted with wax for some South American port, for church purposes, as the large wax candles would indicate. The monogram was cut on this piece for pastime, I have no doubt, by one of the sailors. The wreck must have occurred in the fifteenth or sixteenth century.

Note:

The wreck of the Hudson's Bay Company bark *Vancouver*

in 1848, somewhere near the entrance to the Columbia River, is listed in Bancroft's appendix.

Thomas Rogers

I have been asked to tell what I know about the inscription-bearing rocks found on the side of Necarney mountain. My attention was first called to these stones while on a pleasure jaunt to the Nehalem country in September, 1897. Our first day out from Garibaldi took us to the residence of Mr. Lovell, who resides one and one-half miles south of Necarney, where we remained over night the guests of this old pioneer and his most worthy wife, now deceased. Our host was in a reminiscent frame of mind that night, and as we sat before the cheerful fire, he told story after story of the beeswax ship, whose strange cargo lies under shifting sands of the Nehalem spit.

This led to several pointed questions in which the old gentleman said he was not up to date on rock ology, but if we would hunt up Mr. P. H. M. Smith, who resided near by, and who had spent the past seven years in hunting for the treasure, as well as his father before him, we could obtain all the necessary data required. This we did, visiting Mr. Smith next morning, who, contrary to expectations, was willing to talk upon the subject, besides showing us several 'genuine' marked stones found by himself in divers places, from the mouth of the Nehalem river to the little wind-locked cove north of Necarney, where the remains of an ancient vessel now lies.

Having ascertained all that Mr. Smith was willing to communicate, we visited the pasture lot in which the chisel-marked stones were lying. These were immediately photographed by the writer, the cut of the "Glyphic Rock of Necarney" embellishing this article herewith. When found, these time and weather-beaten stones, four in number, were lying three or four feet deep in the ground in the shape of a huge cross, thirty feet in length by twenty feet in width. Since the first was found, some twenty years ago…these stones, however, Mr. Smith said, did not, in his way of thinking, relate to the treasure – the keystone having been found by him a quarter of a mile distant, buried to the depth of ten feet in the ground on top of a hill southeast. (Clarke, Bowlby, Hobson, and Rogers, *North Pacific Pre-Historic Wrecks*, vol. 2, 219-227. Also see in *Oregon Native Son, Beauty, Beeswax and Rum*, by T. A. Wood, and *The Pirates Treasure Chamber*, by Thomas Rogers)

Note: There is a description of "an ancient wreck" which could be seen at the foot of Neahkahnie Mountain, but was impossible to reach. A storm in 1894 sent portions of this old wreck floating northwards to Arch Cape. The piece of wreckage was picked up by a Mr. Clutrie and taken to the "Astoria Daily Budget" that published a sketch of the ship timber on April 21, 1894, and seen on p. 183, in *Oregon Shipwrecks*.

Don Marshall, the author, described the timbers as "red cedar," fourteen feet long by thirty-two inches wide and seven inches deep. The planks were put together by iron clamps and nails with wooden pins, at four foot intervals, with a tongue on one end, made to fit into a similar grooved plank.

O. F. Stafford

The following description is from *The Oregon Historical Quarterly*, vol. 9, March – December 1908, "The Wax of Nehalem Beach," by O. F. Stafford:

The mountain "spreads out within a distance of two or three miles into a flat, sandy spit which serves to separate Nehalem Bay from the Pacific. Here is a spot not only beautiful in its surroundings, but rich in mysterious legends of shipwreck and buried treasure, as well as vague traditions regarding the first comings of white men to the great Northwest. There are now, to be sure, no certain relics of the shipwrecks, and about all that remains to recall the traditions are occasional pieces of wax, rescued from the sands of the spit, perchance, by a passer-by."

Horace S. Lyman, in his *History of Oregon*, gives an interesting discussion of the first appearances of white men upon the Oregon coast a preserved in Indian traditions. His main authority is Silas B. Smith, an intelligent half-breed, whose mother was a daughter of the Clatsop chief, Kobaiway. Mr. Smith made a special study of the traditions of his mother's people, as a result of which he assigns the earlier comings of white men to three separate occasions, the second of which was the wrecking of a vessel near Nehalem.

To quote from Lyman:

> The Indians state that ship of the white men was driven ashore here and wrecked. The crew, however, survived, and reaching land lived for some time with the natives. A large part of the vessel's cargo was beeswax. But in the course of several months the white men became obnoxious to the Indians because of violating their marital relations. The whites were consequently killed, but fought to defend themselves with slungshot. As Mr. Smith notes, this would indicate that they had lost their arms and ammunition.

"This account, it is to be observed, agrees essentially with the details given by Henry.References to the wax other than those just given are rather infrequent until recent times. Belcher, an early navigator, obtained some specimens in 1837. It is said that six tons of wax from the mouth of the Columbia were received at a Hawaiian port about 1847. Professor George Davidson, of the United States Coast and Geodetic Survey, while at Cape Disappointment in 1851, obtained a specimen which had been picked up on Clatsop beach. Later, in the Coast Pilot for California, Oregon and Washington Territory, 1869, Professor Davidson describes the wax deposit and evidences of the wreck from which it supposedly came. Others to refer to the subject are C. W. Brooks, in a paper before the California Academy of science, 1875, and H. M. Davis, in a communication to the American Antiquarian Society, April, 1892.

During this whole period of eighty years extending from 1813 to 1893 no one seems to have questioned that the deposit of wax was due to any other cause than the thing traditionally accepted as its origin – a wrecked vessel. The only difference of opinion apparent in the matter was regarding the nationality of the vessel, some investigators having it of Spanish ownership, others of Chinese or Japanese."

An article from Judge J. Wickersham, of Tacoma, Washington, who shows by reference to the writings of Brooks, Davidson, and Davis that many shipwrecks of Oriental vessels actually have occurred upon American shores and that therefore a wreck as the source of the wax was at any rate within the limits of possibility. He also calls attention to an error made in the information to Mr. Merrill regarding the amount of wax that had been recovered – no such quantities as those mentioned were ever found."

"Among other duties assigned during the summer of 1895 to Dr. J. S. Diller, one of the ablest field geologists of the United States Geological Survey, was an investigation of this problem. Dr. Diller made his findings public through a letter to the Morning Oregonian of March 27, 1896. This letter is not only the most authoritative discussion ever published upon the subject of Nehalem wax, particularly as regards its geological aspects, but also deals so tritely with some of the other points at issue that a number of paragraphs are bodily reproduced here. Dr. Diller says:

During a trip from Astoria southward along the coast the only place were we found fragments of the wax was near the mouth of the Nehalem. At this point it occurs buried in the deep sand just above the present high tide limit. From the accumulated sediments of the river the beach is gradually growing seaward, and not many generations ago the sea reached the place now occupied by the wax. Mr. Edwards, who was my guide at the place, showed me the stakes marking the areas already dug over by himself in obtaining almost three tons of wax. It was found in the deep sand within ten feet of the surface. He expected to continue working later in the summer, but regarded the locality as almost 'mined out.' We picked up a number of smaller fragments coated with sand, and he showed me others previously collected. Among the latter were several short, cylindrical, hollow pieces like candles from which the wick has disappeared. A few larger pieces weighing from fifty to seventy-five pounds were found some years ago by Mr. Edwards, and also by Mr. Colwell. They bore marks apparently of trade. As the large pieces had all been disposed of I was unfortunately unable to study these marks. The beeswax has been found some miles up the Nehalem river, but always, so far as I could learn, close to the high tide limit. From the Nehalem beach it has been spread along the coast southward by the strong seabreezes of summer, and northward by the storms of winter.

There are two coal fields on the Nehalem, one in Columbia county, and the other in Clatsop near the mouth of the Nehalem, but nothing whatever occurs in either field which resembles the wax, and it is evident from the location of the body of the wax that it was not derived from the adjacent land, but was transported in a body by the sea and dumped not far from its present position.

Its mode of occurrence and the marks upon it clearly indicate that the material is not a natural product of Oregon, but they do not prove that it is wax and not ozokerite brought from elsewhere. The two substances, although very similar in their general composition, are readily distinguishable by chemical tests. Mr. H. N. Stokes, one of the chemists of the Geological Survey, to whom it was referred for examination, says:

> The substance is question is sharply distinguished from ozokerite and other paraffins by its easy decomposition by warm, strong sulphuric acid, and by being saponified by boiling with alcoholic potash, giving soaps which dissolve in hot water, and from which acids throw down insoluble fatty acids. In view of this behavior the material is evidently wax and not ozokerite.

Its melting point, determined by Mr. Stokes, is 64 degrees,

centigrade, which corresponds to that of beeswax and distinguishes it from wax of other kinds known to trade.

A summary of the evidence presented by Dr. Diller shows conclusively that the wax deposit is confined, so far as is known, to a single locality, the Nehalem spit, and that fragments found up the Nehalem, or scattered along the coast, might easily be accounted for as incidental drift; that a few generations ago the sea reached the place now occupied by the wax, that the wax is not derived from the adjacent land; and finally, that although these considerations show only that the wax must have been deposited upon the beach from the ocean, and therefore give no light upon the question as to its nature, chemical tests show decisively that it is not ozokerite, but beeswax."

Another record "concerning recovery of wax is a notation by J. J. Gilbert, of the United States Coast and Geodetic Survey, who made the survey of this part of the coast. He learned that early settlers had plowed the site of the old wreck and obtained 450 pounds of the wax, which was sold as beeswax. Dr. Diller's guide and informant, Mr. Edwards, is said to be no longer living, so that further testimony from him is not available. He is accredited, however, by all old residents of the Nehalem country, from whom it has been possible to get an opinion, with having taken out by far a greater amount of the wax than any other person. Mr. Edwards' own estimate of the amount of wax obtained by him, as he gave it to Dr. Diller, was 'almost three tons.' Mr. D. S. Boyakin, at present and for many years past a resident of Nehalem, and who as a merchant has kept in close touch with traffic affairs of all sorts in that locality, estimates that Edwards and other active wax gatherers known to him have secured in all not much over four tons. This, added to the six tons that may have been shipped to Hawaii in 1847, gives ten tons. Another ton or two for Indian traffic, etc., probably places a liberal estimate upon the whole amount recovered. It is almost impossible to find a piece of the wax upon the beach at the present time, and the consensus of opinion among those most expert in finding it is that the deposit is practically exhausted. The available facts, then, are not incompatible with the wreck hypothesis as far as the amount of wax to be considered is concerned."

Galleons and Junks

"It is not only beeswax with which we are concerned, but beeswax from the Orient. The suggestion that the wrecked vessel was engaged in the carrying trade between the Philippines and Mexico is by no means a new one. Professor Davidson, who for half a century has been actively engaged in material to prove or disprove the existence of the Davidson Inshore Eddy Current along the Northwestern coast, is our highest authority upon the matter of what the sea casts up on these shores. In a recent letter he says:

> My present belief is that the wax is from a wrecked galleon which, by stress of weather on her voyage from the Philippines, had been driven farther north than the usual route. They frequently got as high as 43 degrees, and I know of one wreck as high as the latitude of the Queniult River, Washington.

Judge Wickersham is also at the present time of the opinion that the wax came from the wreck of a Spanish vessel bound from the Philippines to Vera Cruz by way of the North Pacific Current (Kuro Shiwo), which, by the way, seems to have been the route universally taken by eastwardly bound vessels.

Dr. Joseph Schafer, professor of history at the University of Oregon, calls attention to two particularly interesting references in connection with the trade relationships existing between the Philippines and Mexico during early times. The first is from Blair and Robertson, "Philippine Islands," Vol. XV, p. 302:

> A Dutch writer of about 1600 in describing the Philippines says, 'They yield considerable quantities of honey and wax.

The second reference is to Morga, long a governor of the Philippines, sailing from there to Mexico in 1603. His writings are considered the most authoritative extant as regards the Philippines of the early period. In describing the trade from the Islands to Mexico he says:

> In these classes of merchandise (brought from Siam and

other parts of the Orient) and in the productions of the Islands – namely, gold, cotton cloth, mendrinaque, and cakes of white and yellow wax – do the Spaniards effect their purchases, investments, an exports for Nueva Espana (Mexico).

If anything more were needed to establish the hypothesis of a wrecked Spanish vessel it would be an authentic account of the wreck itself. Since the only account known is the one preserved in Indian tradition, we are denied such a crowning bit of evidence. We do have, however, the knowledge that exactly such wrecks did occur. In a reference kindly supplied by Professor Davidson, Venegas' *History of California*, Vol. II, p. 388, there is an account of the wreck of the San Augustin in Drake's Bay, 1595, where was left 'great quantities of wax and chests of silk. (Stafford, *Oregon Historical Quarterly*, 1908, 24-41)

Nehalem Peninsula from Neahkahnie Mountain. (author photo)

S. J. Cotton

The Beeswax Ship

"Romance plays an important part in the story of Nehalem. No part of the coast of Oregon breathes so much of mystery or holds the mind of the story teller so completely in its spell as this. It is, beyond all else, a series of stories so completely baffling that the mind of an Irving would be lost in the skein of unraveled tales. A suggestion here, a hint there, and an unconnected bit of evidence over yonder leads the lover of romance into a maze of possibilities until bewilderment confuses the entire story. There is just enough of realism surrounding the beaches of Nehalem to make any story possible and, to please the mind of the fanciful, writers have indulged their imaginations in wonderful plays, drama and grand operas to such an extent that no history of this section is complete without these stories; a sort of mythology connecting the unrecorded past with the present.

No story had more conflicting details, nor so many doubts surrounding it as that of a ship laden with beeswax which was wrecked upon the long finger of sand stretching from the north mainland and separating Nehalem Bay from the Pacific Ocean. The earliest stories brought down to us by the Indians are replete with incidents connected with it and the early white settlers placed a great deal of confidence in these tales. That a ship carrying much beeswax was wrecked here is without question. No story of the Nehalem country has ever been told without reference to it and all these are substantiated by the immense quantity of wax found scattered along the beach.

The wax has been found in the sands forming the seawall from near Neah-Kah-Nie Mountain to a point three miles toward the Nehalem River. The first white settlers say there were great chunks, some weighing as high as two hundred pounds, either partially buried by the sand or completely under ground. They varied from this size to small candle-shaped pieces, evidently intended for use in the missions along the southern coast. The Indians tell of a greater extent to which it was found. Mrs. Gervais tells of the time when she was a small girl when the beach was strewn for miles with this wax. She frequently visited the beach and found many candles and gathered them with which to play. They had the 'rope' in them, she asserts, meaning that the wicking had not completely rotted away. This was more than three-quarters of a century ago. Her brother was in the habit of packing much of the wax with him on each visit to Astoria, where he sold it to the stores.

But whence came this great amount of wax? This is a part of the romance. Many different stories have been told, but that secured from the last of the natives and one upon which the most reliance can be placed, connects the coming of the beeswax with the equally interesting mystery surrounding the treasure said to have been buried on the sides of Neah-Kah-Nie Mountain, and which will be told in the following story. Even the romancer has taken a hand at the wonderful tale, and added the air of piracy to it. Whether the fated ship, whose bones have partially rotted on the sands of the beach, was navigated by pirates, or whether it was one on a peaceful mission to the Orient, will never be known. Large quantities of teakwood have been found on the beach near the scene of the wreck, but whether this is a part of the wax and treasure ship, or of some other unfortunate craft, is still a mystery. Should this wood have been a part of the ship, its origin must have been in the Oriental countries, as this almost indestructible product of nature is found chiefly n the forests of the Philippine Islands. But the source of the ship and whence it was bound is not particularly a part of our story.

One tale, told to an early settler by Indians residing here, brings three ships in deadly conflict off the Nehalem Beach. It claims the natives were hunting on the slope of Neah-Kah-Nie when they noticed three strange craft far out in the water. As they neared the shore, the watchers could see that the ships were throwing smoke at each other. 'Poof, poof,' is one way in which they described it, and throwing smoke was another. The battle continued for some time and, at last, two of the ships sank. The other was badly damaged, and forced to make the beach for repairs. The native mathematicians figured a crew of thirty men aboard the boat. As soon as the repairs were completed, the ship was pulled from the beach and an attempt made to run it through the breakers. It was a fatal attempt, for it was wrecked before the outer breaker had been reached, and the beach was soon strewn with its equipment. But this latter ship was not the one carrying the beeswax. It was the mysterious treasure ship from which came the story found in the following chapter. The wax was a part of one of the ships which was sunk during the battle.

The story told by Mrs. Gervais, and confirmed by stories told by other natives in years gone by, brings but one ship here. Its nature and the place from which it sailed is still hidden in the distant past. One morning the natives went to the hunting ground along the mountain in quest of game. To their surprise, they found a large quantity of a strange substance; something they had never seen before. It was the beeswax of our story. A little further along on the beach they discovered the wreck of a monstrous 'canoe.' None of them had ever seen an object of this kind before. Its sails were flying in the wind, and objects of every description, new to the Indians, were found on the beach. To add more mystery to the whole affair, there was a number, told to have been thirty, of men whose faces were white and whose dress and language was new to them. By signs, they learned the men had come from across the ocean and their ship had been wrecked during the night.

The date of the wreck is thought to have been about the year 1679. Markings on the wax seem to indicate this assumption is correct. Many pieces have been found with figures, both Roman numerals and Arabic, of this date. One of these, with the date 1679, is now in possession of the Nehalem Valley Bank. The last of the Indians, in relating the story, said she heard the story from her father; it had been told to him by his grandmother, and she heard it from her grandmother. This would carry the story back for four generations of the Indian life, and bring the date not far from that cut upon the chunk of wax recovered.

Many conflicting stories have been told of what became of the crew of this strange vessel. All stories agree that the number was not more than thirty. Some claim the men were all lost while they were trying to rescue a part of the cargo of the wreck, but again we are forced to go back to the most authentic story told by the Indians. Of the number, four are said to have taken the trail to the north, and probably made their way to the vicinity of the Columbia River, where they might have been picked up by a vessel landing there. The remaining twenty-six decided to cast their lot in the beautiful country surrounding the mountain. They built cottages on the slope overlooking the ocean, and attempted to continue the friendly relation with the Indians that had started when they were wrecked. This intercourse did not remain friendly very long. Depredations upon the honest and innocent inhabitants of the country caused ill feeling. Finally their actions became so unbearable that a battle was fought between the white men and the natives in which all the whites were killed.

Previous to the complete destruction of the ship, the men are said to have taken a heavy 'box' far up on the slope of the mountain and buried it. This box, as the Indians described it, is the famed treasure chest of the following story:

The Treasure Ship

Indian narrative brings to us a story hinting of buried treasure on the slope of Neah-Kah-Nie Mountain…The story, as told by Mrs. Gervais, accounts for only one ship, and that carried both the mysterious cargoes. Whether it was a pirate vessel or one destined for the Orient, or from the Orient, will always remain a mystery. Weird tales of piracy have frequently crept into the story. Some claim it was laden with treasure stolen from the churches of Mexico, South America and Oriental countries. According to the most authentic story from the Indian ancestors, there was only one chest taken to the hiding place on the mountain side.

Many men have been engaged in the hunt for the treasure and, as a result, several indications of visits from white men in the centuries past have been found. Not far from the shore, and near the Tavern, the hotel conducted by S. G. Reed, owner of the mountain and adjoining property, is a rock upon which strange markings have been found. Most of these markings were put there a long time ago, and offered the first hint to the earliest searchers, a clue to the hidden gold. This rock weighs more than two hundred pounds and could not have been placed there by some mischievously inclined individual, because it is too much of a load for a practical joke. On the flat surface of the rock the mysterious characters were chiseled. The letter W with a cross on each side, the letters D E with eight dots beside them, and below all an arrow pointing to the slope of the mountain are the first of the keys discovered by the hunters with which they hoped to unlock the secret. A short distance from this rock, a smaller one was found with an arrow and two dots, the arrow pointing to the larger rock mentioned above.

Farther up the slope of the mountain other rock markings have been found, all of which are thought to be associated with those discovered nearer the beach. Pat Smith, one of the hunters devoting the greatest amount of time in quest of the treasure, found a rock buried on the mountain side not far from the higher markings, upon which a plat had been cut." (Cotton, 1915, 45-47)

Note:

Mrs. Gervais, one of the daughters of Chief Coboway was named Margaret and was the sister of Celiast, Mrs. Solomon Smith. She became the wife of Joseph Gervais, when they married in 1839 and they had six children. Mr. Gervais came to Oregon with the Astor Overland Expedition led by Wilson Price Hunt in 1811. He settled on French Prairie in 1830, where his home became the meeting place of the settlers and the location for the first school in Oregon, taught by Solomon Smith. The town of Gervais is named for him.

Alex Walker of the Tillamook County Pioneer Museum, holding the "67" block of beeswax on Manzanita beach in 1955. (Ben Maxwell photo. Salem Public Library Historic Photograph Collection)

Warren Vaughn

Warren Vaughn was an early settler in the Tillamook country, arriving in 1852. His memories of that period were written in the 1890's and published in 2004, in "Till Broad Daylight." He worked with men who settled the Tillamook area; men like Joe Champion, Hiram Smith, Henry W. Wilson, Philip Gearhart, Isaac Alderman, Elbridge Trask, John Hobson, Nathan Dougherty, John Tripp, Truman Harris, and Chief Kilchis.

Henry Wilson, for whom the Wilson River is named, was an English printer who entered the Oregon coast country as a bachelor. He herded the first cows to Tillamook, driving them all the way from Astoria, thus the beginning of the Tillamook dairy industry. He worked at the "Statesman" in Salem in 1853 and was believed to have assisted in the formation of the bill to the Territorial legislature that created Tillamook County. He was also a Democratic representative in Salem for Tillamook County in 1857.

Elbridge Trask was born in Massachusetts and came to Oregon on Nathaniel Wyeth's brig *May Dacre* in 1834. He settled on Clatsop Plains in 1843 and worked at Hunt's Mill, near Astoria. He moved to Tillamook County in 1852, where he worked as a blacksmith and taught school at night. He married Hanna Able, and they had 10 children. The Trask River is named for him.

Philip Gearhart was a pioneer cannery owner and farmer from Pennsylvania. He arrived in Oregon in 1848 and like so many others, took a donation land claim in 1850. He opened the first fish cannery at present day Gearhart and the first sawmill on the coast.

Mr. Vaughn begins by saying that Chief Kilchis was a large man with African features. He was a brave honest leader, and was a descendent of the beeswax ship. The survivor of the vessel was a blacksmith, called a 'chickamin' by the native people, and much like Konapee, taught them how to make knives from the iron of the ship. He married a young woman from the tribe, and Chief Kilchis was one of his descendents.

The legend of the Beeswax ship was told to Mr. Vaughn by an elderly native couple, who were both blind, with hair as white as snow. He believed the ship was from a Catholic society (The San Francisco Xavier was named for Saint Francis Xavier, a priest of the Society of Jesus, the Jesuits) sailing from the West Indies or from Spain, with beeswax destined for the missions in California.

The first to discover the beeswax in the area was a man named Baker, Vaughn said, who arrived in 1864. He built a home on the south side of the Nehalem River and gathered together five to six hundred pounds of the ship's cargo, and then moved away, never to be seen again. (Vaughn, 2004, 22.)

The "Morning Star II" a replica of the original ship, built for the Oregon Bicentennial celebration in 1959. (author photo)

Mr. Vaughn heard of a shipwreck from John Hobson, sometime between 1843 and 1846. Hobson first related that it was a British man-of-war, and then later learned that the name of the vessel was the *Shark*, an American Naval schooner. Pieces of the hull and part of her decks drifted down to Arch Cape. Vaughn saw two cannons there in the sand; one was a brass six-pounder, and the other was a nine pound iron gun. (Vaughn, 2004, 49)

The United States Navy sent the schooner *Shark*, under the command of Lieutenant Neil Howison, to the Columbia River in

1846, to support Astoria, during the boundary dispute between America and Britain. As the ship approached the Columbia, she was met by a lone man in a small canoe, who offered his service as a pilot. He had been a sailor aboard the *Peacock*, five years earlier, which wrecked in 1839, on the north entrance to the River, now known as Peacock Spit. The *Shark* proceeded to hit a sandbar but was eventually moved off to safe water. The next day, the pilot and local pioneer John Lattie was employed to replace the sailor from the *Peacock*. He successfully maneuvered the stuck vessel through the shifting channels into the Columbia. After completing surveys of the lower river, the commander weighed anchor and sailed on September 10, 1846, this time without the guidance of an experienced river pilot. He immediately struck a shoal at the entrance, where the heavy breakers began pounding the vessel. He ordered the crew to lighten the ship, beginning with 12 cannons, and to cut down the three masts. As the *Shark* began breaking up, he ordered; "Abandon ship." The entire crew jumped overboard and made it safely to shore. A terrible storm with high winds blew all night and scattered the wreck, with a large portion floating over the bar and then south. A large piece of wreckage with a cannon and the capstan, came to rest near Cannon Beach.

The settlers in the Tillamook Bay area, heard from the Indians of the ship's remains near Cannon Beach. Mr. Vaughn and a companion traveled to the site, to obtain the iron from the *Shark*, which was used to build the *Morning Star*, the first ship built in Tillamook country. A replica of the original, the *Morning Star II*, was built for the Oregon Bicentennial celebration in 1959 and now rests at the entrance to the Tillamook Cheese Factory.

One of the earliest pioneers, John Gerritse, a sailor whose relatives built ships in Holland, hauled the cannon from the *Shark* out of the ocean, in 1898, with his team of horses and the help of a friend, James Austin. The cannon was set on a foundation at the Rudolph Kissling home, where it remained until it was moved to the entrance of the city of Cannon Beach.

Mary Gerritse, met her future husband, John, one day in a mountain pasture, while she was rounding up the family cows. She saw three men coming from Seaside to Nehalem, and one of the hikers was John, a young Dutch sailor, who left his ship in Astoria, to settle in America.

Mary was 15 years old in 1887 and living in Manzanita, when four treasure hunters came to live with her family. She said they had no luck in finding the treasure. Mary started carrying the mail on horseback around Neahkahnie Mountain in 1897, over the narrow Indian trail, and she continued the service daily from Nehalem to Hug Point until 1904, when the couple moved to Seaside. The mail carrier delivered letters to old leather bags hung on posts from horseback in winter and by wagon in the summer.

The cannon and capstan from the U. S. Naval Survey schooner Shark, at Cannon Beach. September 1960. (Ben Maxwell photo. Salem Public Library Historic Photograph Collection)

Frances Fuller Victor

A guide led the famous historian-adventurer, Frances Fuller Victor, on a short tour of Astoria and around the mouth of the Columbia River in 1871, which she described in "All Over Oregon and Washington." She arrived on a steamer operated by the North Pacific Transportation Company and visited the lighthouse at Cape Disappointment. From there she ventured across the mouth of the river aboard the little steamer *U. S. Grant*, which ran between the lighthouse and Astoria, with the mail for the garrison at Fort Stevens. She also traveled aboard the *Dixie Thompson*; "The elegant steamer which plies between Astoria and Portland."

"Having satisfied ourselves of the material prospects of the town, let us take a friendly guide, and go upon an exploring expedition on our own account. We want to go on foot around the point, by the trail through the woods: but, no; our guide says we must not attempt it, the trail is in such a condition! 'It is low tide, and we will go by the beach.'

"By the beach we go, the, stopping now and then to fillip a jelly-fish back into the water on the end of our *alpenstock*. A beach, indeed! We had always thought that sand, or fine gravel, at least, was essential to that delightful thing in Nature – a beach. But here are *bowlders*, growing larger and larger as we near Young's Bay, until just at the extremity of the point they require much exertion to scramble over. But our guide is entertaining, which compensates for great exertion.

In stories of 'peril by land and water,' of shipwrecks, and legends of treasure-trove – that should be – he drowns all thoughts of mutiny, and we toil ahead. 'To be sure there have been wrecks at the mouth of the Columbia – a century – two centuries ago.' Then he takes from his pocket, where he must have placed it for this purpose, and shows to us a thin cake of beeswax, well sanded over, which he avers was a portion of the cargo of a Japanese junk, cast ashore near the Columbia in some time out of mind. When we have wondered over this, to us, singular evidence of wrecking, he produces another in the form of a waxen tube. At this we are more stultified than before, and then are told that this was a large wax candle, such as the Japanese priest,

84

as well as the Roman, uses to burn before altars. The wick is entirely rotted out leaving the candle a hollow cylinder of wax.

By this self-evident explanation, we are convinced. Certain it is that for years, whenever there had been an unusually violent storm, portions of this waxen cargo are washed ashore, ground full of sand. As bees-wax is a common commodity in Japan, we see no reason to doubt that this, which the sea gives up from time to time, originally came from there . The supposition is the more natural, as the mouth of the Columbia is exactly opposite the northern extremity of that Island Empire; and a junk, once disabled, would naturally drift this way. The thing has been known to occur in later years; and that other wrecks, probably Spanish, have happened on this coast, is evidenced by the light-haired and freckle-faced natives of some portions of it farther north, discovered by the earliest traders."

After an hour of travel they moved inland which "brings us to a pretty piece of level, grassy land away from the beach, where are lofty trees, and lower thickets of wild roses, white spiraea, woodbine, and mock-orange." A little further along and they come to a Clatsop Indian lodge made of cedar planks, with a cedar roof and a number of residents: "Two pretty girls, of ten and twelve years of age, with glorious great, black, smiling eyes." Inside they met with three women, braiding baskets, and two men, surrounded by salmon – hanging from overhead, on the walls, and smoking over a slow fire.

They bid adieu to the local people they have met and continue their journey.

"Our guide points out to us the peculiar features of Young's Bay, and the adjoining country. While we admire again the peaks of Castle Mountain, we listen to a legend, or tradition, which the Nehalem Indians relate of a vessel once cast ashore near the mouth of their river, the crew of which were saved, together with their private property, and a box which they carried ashore, and buried on Mount Neah-carny, with much care, leaving two swords placed on it in the form of a cross." Mrs. Victor also adds the additional twist to the legend, that the chest was buried along with one member of the crew. "The tale corresponds with that told by the Indians of the upper Columbia, who say that some shipwrecked men, one of whom was called Soto, lived two or three years with their tribe, and then left them to try to reach the Spanish countries overland. It is probably enough that a Spanish galleon may have gone ashore near the mouth of the Columbia and it agrees with the character of the early explorers of that nation, that they should undertake to reach Mexico by land. That they never did, we feel sure, and give a sigh to their memory.

Some treasure-seekers have endeavored to find the hidden box, but without result. Casting backward glances at the beautiful mountains, with their romantic foreground of forest and river, we turn toward Astoria...When we reach the point of the peninsula again – Point of Bowlders, we should call it – we are just in time to witness the golden changes of the sunset over Cape Hancock, and to see an ocean steamer coming in. She has passed Fort Stevens, and, by the time we have clambered over rocks and drift-wood to a smoother portion of the beach, is abreast of us, and almost within a stone's throw. We wave our handkerchiefs wildly, knowing, by experience, how pleasant is any signal from the land when our ship is coming in." (Victor, 1872, 50-54)

About the Author: Frances and her sister Metta Victoria, attended a girl's school at Wooster and then traveled to New York to seek literary careers. They were writing for the publications of Rufus Wilmot Griswold, who edited their joint "Poems of Sentiment and Imagination, with Dramatic and Descriptive Pieces," 1851. Frances married the naval engineer Henry Clay Victor, in 1862, and his brother, Orville James Victor, married her sister. In 1863, her husband was ordered to San Francisco and there she contributed to various newspapers. In 1865, the Victor's moved to Oregon, where she developed a tremendous enthusiasm for the Pacific Northwest. Her first books on the history of the Northwest were "River of the West," 1870, and "All Over Oregon and Washington," 1872. After she lost her husband in the wreck of the *Pacific*, 1875, she joined the staff of Hubert Howe Bancroft and wrote part of the "History of the Northwest Coast," 1884, and all of the "History of Oregon," 1886. She also completed other historical works on the West.

Treasure
Nehalem Treasure

Bill Burrud Productions of KTTV, Los Angeles, aired a series of documentaries, beginning in October of 1958, under the title "Treasure." The first broadcast was the tale of The Lost Dutchman Mine, from the Superstition Mountains, in Arizona, the Neahkahnie Treasure story was the second.

The location crew for the "Treasure" series flew into Nehalem in early September 1957, and made, what was described as a spectacular landing on the beach, during a high tide and high winds. The crew began filming with a flight over Neahkahnie Mountain. Additional scenes in the documentary program highlighted the various treasure rocks, and pits that were dug around the mountain, pieces of beeswax owned by local residents, and a shot of a Manila galleon model on the beach.

The writer, Eb Giesecke, was invited by the production company to be the historical adviser for the story, and he also appeared in a segment for the program explaining the legends of the treasure ship. (Giesecke, *Oregonian*, 1957)

The silver holy oil receptacle created by Dutch silversmiths, taken from the hull of a shipwreck on the Nehalem Spit by John E. Tuttle in 1898. (Ben Maxwell photo. Salem Public Library Historic Photograph Collection)

Nehalem Shipwreck

Harry Tuttle was four years old, in 1898, when his father John E. Tuttle, drove the family to Nehalem Beach in their horse and buggy. While beachcombing the spit, during an extremely low tide, they saw two old ship's masts shooting up from out of the sand. At the site of the shipwreck they dug out beeswax, some with inscriptions, and a solid silver container. In 1941, the container was sent to the Smithsonian Institution for examination, where the experts concluded it was made by Dutch silversmiths. The hallmark on its lid was used for silver pieces in several European cities, but particularly in Utrecht, Holland, around 1750. (Hult, 1971, 105.)

The receptacle was used as a container for holy oil, which would have been carried by early Franciscan and Jesuit missionaries. The holy oil receptacle is on display at the Tillamook County Pioneer Museum and was received through a grant from First Interstate Bank in 1988. It was actually recovered from the hull of the shipwreck on the Nehalem Spit in 1898, by John E. Tuttle. According to the information at the Museum, the receptacle was made by Dutch silversmiths in the early 1700s:

Holy Oil Receptacle

This small Holy Oil receptacle was found in the hull of a shipwreck on the Nehalem Spit in 1898 by John E. Tuttle. It is believed to be of Dutch origin and crafted in the early 1700s. The vessel is 5.4 centimeters tall and 4 cm at its maximum diameter. Constructed of solid silver, the "O" on the lid is thought to stand for "oleum" indicating it was a container for sacred oil. While this form of vase has existed since the 17th century, they were still in use until the late 19th century. There were probably three vessels for all three kinds of sacred oils brought on board the ship by a Franciscan monk or priest.

In the "Research Design for the Beeswax Wreck Project" Scott Williams says the silver oleum jar was a design from the 17th century, "possibly second half and later."

Ben Lane holding an inscribed piece of beeswax and a candle at Nehalem in August 1954. (Ben Maxwell photo. Salem Public Library Historic Photograph Collection)

Thomas Rogers said he saw the Nehalem shipwreck exposed in the sand in 1896: "In 1896, the late T. B. Handley of Tillamook told me by long distance telephone that the lowest tide in 20 years was on, that the hull of the ship was exposed, and he urged me to come at once. I hastened to Neah-kah-nie only to find that I was so late that we could get but an occasional glimpse of the ship, which was so deep in the sand that the sea broke over it. A friend, however, had anticipated us by taking a wooden pulley and some teak wood from the wreck."

The Horner Museum at Oregon State University displays the pulley recovered from the wreck by the friend of Mr. Rogers. It is 32 inches long, made of teak, and was carbon-dated to the mid 1600's.

The book "Nehalem" by Rogers, was inspired by "the discovery of a large chunk of beeswax on the sandspit north of Cape Meares many years ago, and a mammoth candle displayed in the office of the Tillamook Headlight." (Horner, 1929, 48-55)

Edmund Halley Lane, a direct descendent of the famous English astronomer, Edmund Halley, collected enough teakwood for three piles, that were stacked as high as his woodshed. He and his brother Jack Lane, from Seattle, combed the beach near the mountain searching for beeswax in 1905. They found a fantastic piece weighing over 125 pounds, with the letter "M" inscribed in the center. Representatives from the Smithsonian and the Oregon Historical Society contacted Mr. Lane, at that time concerning his discovery. (Lane, 1972, 156)

Pat Smith removed several pieces of teak that prompted the British Vice Consul, at Astoria, E. M. Cherry, to plan a salvage of the wreck in 1929, which he eventually abandoned due to the $30,000 expense for a coffer dam. Mr. Cherry's interest in the sunken ship was reported in the "Morning Oregonian," Thursday, August 1, 1929. It stated that the ship was buried in the sands, and the ribs of the hull were visible when the wind blew away the covering sands.

A number of pieces from the timbers, exposed in the sand, were cut away in the 1930's, by Ben Lane, the mayor of Manzanita. From these he built a small table, now on display at the Columbia River Maritime Museum in Astoria. A sample of the table was tested at the Department of Wood Science and Technology, at the University of Washington, in 1970. Dr. L. Leney determined that the wood was "teak," from the Malaya or Philippine Islands. Pieces of this wood are also displayed at the Tillamook County Pioneer Museum. (Marshall, 1984, 178)

The treasure hunter Pat Smith, salvaged teakwood planks from the vessel, and helped finance his explorations, by selling canes made from the hardwood.

"For some years past Pat Smith, the well known delver for hidden treasure on Necarney mountain has salvaged sticks of teakwood timber from the hull of an old wreck on Necarney beach, and having sawed them into convenient lengths of canes, has disposed of them at a nominal price as souvenirs. The wreck is only accessible at very low tide, and most of the time it is buried under huge deposits of ocean sands. When the currents are right, however, and the tide is also low, it can be seen and gotten to. There is much speculation as to this wreck, but the fact that the hull or portions of it at least were composed of teakwood, gives arise to the idea that it may have been a Chinese junk . How long ago it was wrecked, and the circumstances attending it, are matters merely of conjecture. There is however, some Indian tradition about it." (Headlight Herald, February 22, 1924)

Note

The teak constructed ship, like most Spanish galleons, was built in the Philippines, quite possibly at Cavite.

Lost Gold Mine

Indians who traded with gold at the store of Col. T. H. Cornelius, in Gales City, near Forest Grove, created the legend of the Lost Indian Gold Mine. In order to find where the natives were getting their gold, local residents followed them into the mountains, west of Gales Creek, but the elusive miners always managed to throw them off track.

F. T. Watrous, who grew up in the Tualatin valley, was told the tales of the Indian gold mine by Sol Emerick, a farmer with 160 acres, on the west Tualatin plains. For many years Emerick heard of a great gold deposit, located somewhere in the mountains, from the Indians who camped near his farm. He and his wife, both wore rings made from nuggets that were given to him by his generous visitors. An elderly native woman revealed where the gold could be found to Emerick before she died, and pointing to the coast range said; "Go three suns to the white mountain, where water runs to a lake in a black canyon you will find it." Sol Emerick searched for a white mountain with a black canyon, with a lake, but never found it.

Mr. Watrous hiked over the mountains to the coast, to meet a woman named Rose, who confirmed the stories of the Indian mine, but was unable to say where it could be found. It was during the time he was searching for clues to the lost mine, that he met a man living next to Hall's reservation store, on the Siletz Indian reservation. This man told Watrous that he wouldn't get much information about the hidden mine there, but then proceeded to tell him a tale of a Portuguese sailor, who was his grandfather. This sailor helped bury five teakwood chests of Portuguese coin, in a creek, somewhere in the Tillamook area.

After a shore party, from a Portuguese ship buried the chests, they were attacked by Indians, leaving only one survivor, who escaped over the coast range to the safety of a homestead owned by a Mr. Iler. After recuperating from his ordeal, he led a group of searchers, with Iler, to uncover the hidden treasure chests, but were unable to locate the lost creek. The castaway then traveled to Fort Vancouver, where he gained passage on a ship to Europe, and eventually returned to his home. He returned to the HBC post on the Columbia with a new wife & young son, and gained employment as a clerk with the trading company. After he was injured in a gunpowder explosion, he was released by the company, and then moved to the coast with his small family, to search once again for the treasure.

The son of the Portuguese sailor married a Nehalem Indian maiden, and their son was the man who told Watrous this story. Mr. Watrous determined that the creek where the chests were buried was north of Manhattan, not far from Rockaway. (Hult, 1971, 97-103) Also see the *Headlight Herald*, Tillamook, Sunday, July 11, 1965. "Legend Reports County Sports Lost Gold Mine."

August Hildebrand, "A Trip to Neah-Kah-Nie, The Treasure Mountain," the Oregon Historical Society, 1926.

The historian August Hildebrand, recalls a hiking adventure from Astoria to Nehalem, which commenced in Astoria, on Saturday, August 8, 1926. In the article he mentions the *Glenesslin* shipwreck of 1913, but also goes on to some details concerning the famous Beeswax Wreck. He begins by saying: "The last wreck that occurred near this cove to the south was the British ship "Glenesslin" which piled up on the rocky coast, with all sails set about 1913. Pirate and smuggler's stories, galore, have a natural setting here that lead to fanciful stories as being real.

The very first authentic wreck occurred near here during the year 1783. (Before the coming of the white man.) It was a Spanish vessel that had beeswax as part of a cargo. This beeswax was in evidence during the writer's early life about forty years ago. It was plowed up or dug up on the sandy beach just south of the Neah-Kah-Nie Mountain. It was then sent to Astoria as a trading article. Tons of it were sent in and some was bought by the historian himself. It was in all kinds of shapes and coated black from the particles of black gold-bearing sand that adhered to it on account of being a somewhat sticky substance. It is supposed that this wax was intended for wax candles in the Catholic churches of Lower California or Mexico. These countries had an earlier civilization than the American Pacific Northwest."

Mr. Hildebrand had "an old friend that knew something about old Indian life and also knew about the treasure." This is what she said: "I am quite old now. My father was a French Canadian trapper. My grandfather also trapped and traveled much. When I was a little girl, say about six years old, I knew of an old Indian woman that visited with my mother. She was from the Tillamook country, that is, all that part that lies south of Tillamook Head. I listened in on their talk. She told my mother that when she was a child they lived at Nehalem, A ship came ashore. This ship was in distress, in need of repairs and was beached . While it was upon the ocean shore, a storm broke and smashed the ship beyond further repair. Everything was taken off. We Indians were frightened. They were people of different looks. They had curly hair while ours was straight. In later years we called them Portuguese. We ran away from them and hid on top of Nie-kah-Nie Mountain behind the rocks. Some people claim that it was gold. We Indians did not know the value of money and did not care. No one was killed over the box, as reported – and we Indians simply left it alone.

At another time this Indian woman asked my mother to visit with her in the Nehalem country. She seemed to like her home and was enthusiastic about the surroundings. She told mother that one wonderful thing that she would like to show her and that was a mountain to the south of Neah-Kah-Nie. This mountain was flat on top like a table. This square piece of land was not large, but near the center was the foot print of a large person. The Indians looked where this person could have walked to but found no other footprints. This person must have stepped from the clouds – on earth and must have gone right at once to heaven again.

At another occasion there were two Indian women visitors – one showed my mother a handful of gold nuggets. My mother said, 'This is gold – it is money – and you can buy many things with it.' The other woman spoke up and said: 'I know where there are lots of rocks like these. Away to the north there is one place about the size of where a wigwam can stand – in the woods – away from the ocean – in thick underbrush. You cannot see anywhere from there. It is a kind of a hole. There are lots of those yellow rocks there." This is quite possibly a reference to the famous Lost Tillamook Mine.

August Hildebrand: "The historian has now given you the secrets of the treasure and gold.

While we are talking or writing about treasures, early Norsemen culture and Indians, the following may interest you: - Many names of mountains and places in the Northwest in British Columbia and Alaska are of supposed Indian origin. This is going back not far enough. The real wise ones know them to be North Chinese names. This would indicate Chinese intercourse long before Columbus discovered America and long, long before Lewis and Clark. The beeswax was traced as coming from China. It is also claimed that many articles in use by the Indians before the event of John Jacob Astor and the Hudson Bay Company were of Chinese origin. At any rate the middle syllable of the word Neah-Kah-Nie means in North Chinese 'head.' The last word means soil or earth. The middle syllable of the word Ne-ha-lem means river, the last means forest. This agrees very well with the physical aspect of the objects.

Neah-Kah-Nie is a headland, promontory with soil, earth, grass, meadows on the Northwest and south slopes.

Nehalem is a river in a forest. Even Til-la-mook is translated as 'brought lumber to us.'

Wa-ha-na can be translated as Union River. It is probably correct as this river forms a union with the Necanicum at Seaside just before both flow into the ocean. Ancient Chinese coins have been found in Alaska and the Japanese and Chinese railroad grade laborers claim that they every once in a while come across rocks and cliffs with Chinese markings.

We again struck the old Neah-Kah-Nie mountain trail. This trail has been in existence since 1870 so far as the white man is concerned. It followed an old Indian trail. It is said that Indians and Elk always had their trails over mountain and hill tops.

We were now ready for the decent and went down the south side on a straight line toward Nehalem Beach…On the beach to the south, which was sandy and full of driftwood, Mr. and Mrs. Huswick, who had preceded us, had prepared coffee. We lunched – and inspected the surroundings which composed several seaside cottages, in a large sea beach hotel, 'Neah-Kah-Nie Inn,' that looked inviting, and a frontier store in which we bought ice cream and the inevitable soda pop. On the way down near the seaside cottages, we passed the famous rocks with the mysterious markings that are supposed to indicate the location of the buried treasure.

We were soon seated in our mountain auto and were rolling along. After a short stop at Seaside, we arrived back at Astoria Sunday about 10 p.m.

Note: Also read Fred Lockley's column Oregon Journal, August 11, 1929 – "Pirate or Merchantman?" There were visiting Portuguese ships to the Northwest Coast in 1788-1789, and again in 1792-1793, listed in Cook's "Flood Tide of Empire" Appendix E, Nationality of Vessels Visiting the Northwest Coast, 1774-1820.

One of the oldest treasure stories from Nehalem was written for the Oregonian and printed on May 29, 1890, "The Buried Nehalem Treasure" which seems to have some correlation to the Portuguese treasure:

In the year 1820, says the Tillamook *Headlight*, it is reported that a Spanish vessel came into Nehalem bay with a large amount of treasure onboard consisting of six boxes of Spanish money, each box requiring six men to move it, and the total value was $1,500,000. The captain being a pirate and closely pursued, put into Nehalem bay, and finding a lonely place, agreed with his crew to bury the money and valuables on a certain side of the river near where a small creek put in, and between two certain trees. They each agreed with their captain by a binding obligation that they would never reveal the place where the treasures were buried, with a penalty of their lives, unless all were agreed and to share the treasures equally.

In the year 1852, one of the survivors, whose life was saved by a man at that time living near Portland, afterwards on a deathbed made the above confession.

Some seventy years had passed away and still this large sum of money lies buried in the shady nook of the Nehalem. Last week the old man came to the town that this confession was made to, and quietly wended his way toward the majestic Nehalem, in pursuit of the long-hidden treasure. This is not the only man that is in search of these buried treasures, but for several years past men have come to Tillamook county and in the vicinity of Nehalem have dug large holes and doubt will reveal many hidden mysteries. But who will find the hidden treasure on the Nehalem river?

17th Century Gold Coins

Spanish gold was found in the walls of an old home near Mohler, which is just a few miles from Manhattan, as reported in *The North Tillamook County News*, April 17, 1936. August Grab, a dairyman in the Tillamook area, found 12 old Spanish coins between the two by fours of an old house he was tearing down in 1936. The largest coins were about the size of an American half dollar, bearing the head of Queen Isabella, and had various dates, close to 1618. Friends and neighbors stopped by to see his incredible discovery. There was no accompanying documentaion with the treasure. The

Grab farm was originally the old Fisher homestead.

Don Viles relates a story of gold coins found near Manhattan, in "Treasure Hunting Northwest," and a quantity of huge candles taken from the edge of a lake, over a hundred years ago, also from the same Manhattan area. (Hult, 1971 107-108.)

Pirates

Thomas Cavendish set sail in 1586, to attack Spanish shipping in the Pacific, with veterans from Drake's voyage. On the way to Panama he also captured a ship and learned from the pilot, Tomas de Ersola, enough information to position his ships near Cape San Lucas, the southernmost point off Baja, and the time of year to intercept the next galleon from Manila. His crew sighted the Manila galleon, *Santa Ana,* on November 15, 1587, and launched the attack. The stout Spanish crew was able to repel four boarding attempts by the English, during two days of battle. The decks of the galleon became scattered with rigging after repeated broadsides, leaving the ship in shambles, forcing the defenders to surrender. The *Santa Ana* turned out to be a fabulous prize for Cavendish, with 122,000 pesos in gold, and a hold full of pearls and silks. The British captain ferried 190 survivors to a nearby shore, and then torched the ship. He then turned west into the Pacific with two ships – the, *Desire*, with the galleon's heavily laden cargo, and an escort the *Content*. At some point they lost sight of the escort, which was last seen moving northward along the Baja coast, and was never seen again, possibly shipwrecked on some lonely windswept beach.

Another English privateer, Woodes Rogers, prowled the Pacific Coast. He seized the Manila galleon, *Nuestra Senora de la Encarnacion* when it passed Cabo San Lucas, in 1709. His squadron had previously captured Spanish vessels off the coast of South America.

The *San Sebastian* was pursued by another Englishman, George Compton in 1754 near Santa Barbara. The galleon's crew purposely ran the ship aground on Santa Catalina Island, to escape the raider.

It is possible that a fleeing Manila galleon being chased by a pirate ship was destroyed off the Oregon coast. A corsair cruising these waters was not an impossibility, according to Warren Cook. He states there were twenty-five privateers, or pirates preying upon ships that sailed the west coast, between 1575 and 1742. There are references in Spanish archives to pirate ships cruising the west coast of Mexico that have never been identified. (Cook, 1973, 37)

Spanish pirates landed at various places along the Pacific coast, according to the authors Ruby & Brown. One Indian tradition recalls the story of a thousand man army, led by "Ractamoos," a Nisqually chief, who engaged a smaller force of four hundred Spanish pirates, at a northern Puget Sound shore. After the battle, one hundred and fifty of the remaining freebooters, were lost in a in a raging storm in the Strait of Juan de Fuca. (Ruby & Brown 1981, 5)

The pirate William Charles Morgan, cruised the pacific coast in his schooner *Inferno* between 1645 and 1657. He was known as "One-eyed Willie," after losing an eye in a battle with the Spanish. Accounts kept in the diaries of British naval officers say that their navy sunk the pirate ship in a bay near Ecola State Park. The *Inferno* was reportedly sunk under a barrage of fallen rocks from cliffs that were bombed by the British. Morgan supposedly survived this battle, living in caves, where legends say he buried his treasure.(Moody, 2006, 113-115)

The legend of an Oriental sailor, who survived a drifting junk, helplessly carried over the Pacific in the Japanese current, was handed down by the Nehalems. He was captured by the natives, but gained his freedom by teaching them how to build boats. He then turned pirate, striking at coastal villages from the Columbia, in the north, to Coos Bay, in the south, with swift war canoes, and became feared along the Oregon coast. (Gibbs, 1971, 106)

Treasure Hunters

In 1880, William Batterson, an early homesteader from California, settled near Neahkahnie mountain, and unearthed several rocks with curious inscriptions. He said that he had found rocks with similar markings in Humboldt County, California, that were survey markers of old Spanish land grants.

Will Snyder hit a boulder while plowing, with a series of designs similar to those found by Hiram Smith at the foot of Neahkahnie Mountain in 1865. Hiram, who was a surveyor by trade, passed his knowledge on to his son Patrick Smith who searched for Spanish treasure, beginning in 1898, that he believed was buried on or near the mountain, or possibly somewhere on the Nehalem beach. He married a native woman who, some say, took him to the spot where it was buried. He was known as the "Hermit of Nehalem" and dedicated fifty years of his life to the search for the Neahkahnie treasure.

Warren Vaughn believed that the Hudson's Bay Company may have beat Smith to the location, stating that if there were treasure to be found, the Hudson's Bay Company, or even Astor's men would have found it long ago. (Vaughn, 2004, 22)

Thomas McKay, the son of Alexander McKay and the stepson of Dr. John McLoughlin, while trapping in the Nehalem area, met an old crone who said she had seen white men come ashore carrying something they buried on the side of Neahkahnie mountain and pointed out the exact spot to him. (Drawson, 1973, 134-139)

He denied finding any treasure when he appeared before company authorities at Fort Vancouver, but he always seemed to have an abundance of money, and was very generous with his neighbors at French Prairie, which started the rumor that he had unearthed a treasure chest.

There was a story of a black man living near The Dalles, Ore. in the early 1800's, who claimed he was one of the men that witnessed the burial of the treasure chest and said he knew exactly where it was. He said he was a castaway, enslaved by a local chief and would never go back there. Unfortunately, he died of smallpox before he could lead an expedition to recover the great treasure. (Gulick, 2002, 76)

Curt Beckham wrote about Pat Smith in "Neah-kah-nie, Mountain of Dreams" for the publication "Oregon Coast" 1990. Smith studied Spanish to prepare himself for a trip to Spain, where he planned to visit the government archives in Madrid, to research the official records in his search for lost galleons. In the archives he read of seven "treasure-laden ships" that had sailed west from Peru to Spain. Two of the ships failed to complete the long, hazardous journey, and Pat believed that one of these could have been the legendary Nehalem shipwreck.

After he returned from Spain, he received a visit from three Spanish engineers, carrying with them an old Spanish survey map, indicating the burial place of an ancient treasure. The key to the map, they believed, was a rock Pat had found many years ago, but he would never reveal the site of its origin to the mysterious Spanish treasure hunters.

Three Rocks Wreck

Just twenty-three miles north of Yaquina Head, at the mouth of the Salmon River, lies the remains of a mysterious ship. About 800 yards offshore are the three rocks for which the legend is now known, Three Rocks Wreck. Early settlers in the area have recalled legends from the Indians of a "white-winged ship" that long ago wrecked here. Evidence of the wreck has been uncovered in the sands and fishermen have repeatedly snagged their nets on some underwater obstruction.

In 1931, while clearing a summer campsite, E. G. Calkins, the landowner at Three Rocks Beach, made a fascinating discovery. While leveling a mound, with his plowshare, he unearthed some Indian relics; a whalebone war club, stone pestles, and a broken iron kettle. Near this mound he picked up an oversize human thighbone. Further probing of the soil produced the entire skeletal remains of a giant, and two normal size skeletons.

Dr. F. M. Carter, a physician, and Oregon historian, Dr. John Horner, were called in to give their expert opinions on the discovery. After his examination, Dr. Carter claimed the bones were of "an eight-foot giant of the Negroid race." The smaller skeletons were believed to be Indians.

Dr. Carter was familiar with the legend of Three Rocks Wreck, a tale of 20 men who came ashore, and reputedly buried a chest, leaving two of the survivors to guard the location, while the other 18 left to explore the coast. One of the guardians was said to be a large black man.

The Indians buried their tribal brothers facing west and their enemies facing east, exactly the way the graves were situated. Dr. Carter, who was the Lincoln County coroner, was familiar with Indians of the area in the late 1800s, and recalled seeing "black Indians with kinky hair."

Mr. Calkins also found evidence of the shipwreck, when he recovered hardwood timbers with copper bolts. His father was gill-netting at the mouth of the Salmon River beginning in 1913, and would tangle his nets on something, just seven feet below the surface, and only a short distance from where the skeletons were found, eighteen years later. Twice after his nets were snagged and pulled free, bits of wreckage were brought up, including a curved section of a ship's rib, with heavily corroded copper nails. (Gibbs, 1978, 31-33, also see the *Oregon Journal,* April 26, 1931)

In "Pirate Gold at Three Rocks Beach" Eb Giesecke says that Mr. Calkins "explored the river bottom, and – Scarcely a dozen feet deep – he found the remains of an old sailing vessel, identified by a double row of rotting ribs." (Giesecke, Oregonian, 1956)

Ed Calkins began collecting evidence in 1973, to present to the State Land Board, for permission to excavate at Three Rocks Beach, where the artifacts were plowed up by his father in 1931. When he visited Oregon State University to locate the items collected by Dr. John Horner, the history professor at the school in the 1930's, he found that they were missing. Dr. Horner was believed to have returned to Corvallis with the artifacts in 1931 where he began a museum named after him.

According to Eve Muss in her Oregon Journal article of March 12, 1977, Dr. Horner gathered together the contents of the shell mound which he took back to Corvallis. The artifacts came up missing along with a 3000 word essay written by the history professor. The missing essay may have included a description of the artifacts and Dr. Horner dated the grave site at 260 to 300 years old, in 1931, using the size of spruce trees that were cleared from the top of the shell mound.

A photograph of Dr. F. M. Carter, Elmer G. Calkins, and Prof. John B. Horner, taken in 1931 at the site of the discovery, was kept by Wallace Broadwell, who was present the day of the excavation. The photo was given to him by the Oregon Journal photograher who took the picture. The photo shows skeletal remains of three men; a whale-bone war club, a box with a spearhead, a crude stone pestle and a broken iron tea kettle.

Calkins said he located the place where the ship went to pieces, just 300 yards from where the artifacts were uncovered. A steel probe outlined a submerged wooden object, approximately 9 feet below the surface. Two wood-working experts stated that core samples taken from the sunken object are a variety of ironwood found only in the Southern Hemisphere. A metal detector designed to register the presence of gold and silver, was active in a particular spot of the Salmon River Estuary, where he was directed by his father.

Mr. Calkins was unfortunately denied a permit from the Army Corps of Engineers in 1974, to dredge an area 70 feet by 30 feet at a 10 foot depth, near the entrance to the Salmon River.

Newport

Goblets of Spanish origin have been recovered from the bottom of Yaquina Bay, and a brass-handled ship's cutlass was found along the shore in Newport, with several copper coins, bearing the inscription, "English Trade Tokens, 1788," a year when Captain Robert Gray sailed the northern coast and entered Tillamook bay. Captain Gray is credited with the discovery of the Columbia River in 1792, 300 years after Columbus discovered America, and named after his ship the *Columbia Rediviva*. (Gibbs, 1971, 108)

Ancient Anchor

An anchor was hoisted aboard the *Margaret E.* from the bottom, just a mile north of the Yaquina Bay sea buoy. Captain Hugh Shaw, of Portland declared that it was definitely from an old sailing ship. The fisherman in the Newport area believe that the 1500 pound anchor, tore away from the end of its anchor chain, which was discovered near the mouth of Beaver Creek, five miles south of Newport. The chain was uncovered by Jim and Mike Earl, also of Newport, while fishing nearby. There are also exposed timbers of an unidentified ship on the sandy shore of Beaver Creek, just a short distance upriver from the old chain.

Some of the residents believe that the seven-foot stock anchor, and chain are from the *Ona*, which wrecked at Beaver Creek in 1870.

There is the possibility that the anchor is from a legendary treasure ship, that was carrying $250,000 in gold coins, which foundered in a cove, that could have been the mouth of Beaver Creek. According to a Yaquina Indian legend, members of the tribe saw the legendary ship attacked by men who they called pirates, then driven ashore and scuttled. (Allyn, Oregonian, 1961)

Silk Laden Ship from China

George Luther Boone, grandson of the famous Kentuckian, Daniel Boone, was living at Yaquina Bay, when Eva Emery Dye interviewed him at his home in February 1905. During the conversation Mr. Boone mentioned the wreck of a silk-laden ship from China, near Yaquina Bay in 1849, which was never identified. He heard the story from Jack Bamber. "In 1864 I helped survey the first road over the Coast Range to Yaquina where the railroad now goes. Before this we had blazed a wagon-road to tide water. In 1870 we built this house for many a long year the best on the coast, and with George Collins, descendant of that Collins who journeyed with Grandfather Daniel into Kentucky

100 years before, we helped hew and haul timber to build the most western lighthouse on the continent.

Not knowing how many vessels have been lost at Yaquina, Jack Bamber said that early in '49 a silk-laden ship from China was wrecked here. The cargo drifted ashore and Coast Indians wore shawls that would have sold for $100 apiece in San Francisco. Bamber's Indian wife had a shawl. She used to wash for us. An Irishman got 1800 yards of silk.

As to the lighthouse – terrific was the toil dragging lumber up that high promontory and building on the rock in a wind that fairly blew the saws out of the men's hands. But it saved many a storm-tossed ship whose distracted master has cried 'See! See! Cape Foulweather Light!' shooting its beams thirty miles out on the water." (Dye, 1941, 220-229)

The ship was most likely the *James Warren* listed in Bancroft's Appendix, which he locates fifty miles south of Tillamook, at Yaquina Bay: "…in 1849, at mouth of the Columbia, the brig *Josephine*; likewise elsewhere and at another time, *Silva de Grace*, and *James Warren*, the latter fifty miles south of Killemook."

Additional Newport News

Julius Schafer of Newport picked up an unusual stone jar, in early March, 1939, from the sands of the large coastal city, stuffed with three $100 bills, and some change. Nobody knows where the money came from. (Oregonian & Oregon Journal, 1939)

Gold Beach

In the 1940s, a farmer's plowing, near Gold Beach, Oregon, was brought to an immediate halt when he hit something in his field, located somewhere between Hwy 101 and the ocean shore. While digging around the plow he removed several pieces of wood, small nails, copper fittings and the remains of leather straps, from what appeared to have been a large wooden trunk, or chest. He also removed some small statues and ornaments made of gold and silver, a number of pieces of jewelry, and Spanish coins! (Jameson, 1995, "The Curious Sir Francis Drake Treasure" 74-78)

Spanish silver coins were found near Gold Beach at Illahe on the Claude Bardon place, in 1933, by Fred McClung, who was placer mining. The three coins, were larger than a dime but smaller than a quarter, with the largest being a "2 real." One was dated 1734, another 1712 and the third 1700.

The coins could have been lost by Spanish miners, according to the Oregonian article, who worked the Rogue River beaches before American settlers arrived. Spanish coins have also been found along the Rogue River, but these were the oldest.

The coins could easily have been dropped by a crewmember of a Spanish ship exploring the bay or searching for water. (*Oregonian*, 1933)

Three and four-masted sailing ships anchored in the Columbia River, ca. 1900. "Ships at Anchor – Astoria, Oregon." (photograher unknown. Ben Maxwell collection. Originally from the Captain Eckhart collection. Salem Public Library Historic Photograph Collection)

Captain Scarborough

Captain James Scarborough came to the rescue of the ship *Brothers of Guernsey* in 1844, when she became stranded on a sand bar, after entering the Columbia. A record of the event was kept in the diary of Rev. George Gary. The minister was sent by the Mission Board of the Methodist Episcopal Church to the Oregon Territory, aboard the *Lawrence* which sailed from New York harbor on November 30, 1843, and arrived at Honolulu, on April 24, 1844. There the passengers boarded the *Brothers of Guernsey* under Captain Flere, for the voyage to Fort Vancouver. They entered the Columbia and began the approach upriver on May 23:

Fri. 24. "This morning our Captain is making a stir to start up the river, but soon a canoe is seen coming toward us; he was persuaded to wait until its arrival. To our great joy it proves to be Mr. Birnie. He informed our Captain of the unfavorable state of the tide and, consequently, we wait a while. As the land is near us, the Captain has some of his men take a boat and take himself and Mr Birnie, Mrs Gary and myself on shore. Here we spend an hour or two and here we are walking on land in Oregon. Vegetation is in a very flourishing state, everything indicates a very strong soil. We return to our vessel and in a favorable state of the tide make an effort to go up the river. Fort Vancouver is about one hundred miles up the river. For vessels to pass up the river it is necessary to move in low tide, then if she strikes the bars, when the tide rises she will float. We spent the day in trying to get up the river and with all care and toil and until twilight. We passed perhaps eight miles. Being about two miles below Fort George, our Captain went home with Mr Birnie.

Sat. 25. Our mate and men, being desirous to show their competency easily hoisted anchor and before the arrival of the Captain and Mr Birnie, spread their sail and made an effort to go up the river; and very soon we are snugly on a sand bar. The Captain and Mr Birnie came and finding the vessel so fast on the bar, our cannon is again fired as a signal to a vessel at anchor at Fort George, for aid. Captain Scharborough and five of his men come to our aid.

About ten a. m. our vessel is afloat again. The Captain and his men remain with us all day and we ascend the river perhaps two miles, so we are near Fort George."

Mon. 27. "This morning while waiting for wind, also tide, and Mrs Roberts being now comfortable, we go on shore and visit Mr Birnie and family, look at the surrounding scenery, no appearance of a fort, we see where the Indian dead have been deposited in their canoes, the bones of some are visible. We saw where the once great and famous Concomly once lay quiet in death…After spending three our four hours on shore very pleasantly, aided and attended by Mr Birnie and family, we return to the boat. In the afternoon an effort is made to progress up the river. We are attended by Mr Birnie, Capt. Scharborough and an Indian pilot called George; though the river is wide, the channel is narrow. The Captains and Mr Birnie are so full of talk and also so full of drink, we touch and stick three times in going four miles, but the tide and wind are in our favor. Soon after we cast anchor for the night, a vessel coming down the river sends us a fat sheep. Mr Roberts, I suppose, has let some persons know what poor and miserable fare we have on board this vessel. Mr Birnie and Capt. Scharborough return to the fort, so we are now left with our Indian pilot." (Carey, OHQ 1923, 74-76)

Although the vessel made the Columbia entrance on May 23, it was not until the last day of the month, that they finally anchored at their destination of Fort Vancouver.

The pioneer-naturalist, James G. Swann wrote about the Captain in 1853, and said that Scarborough Hill was "one of the most prominent objects seen while entering the Columbia. Captain James Scarborough, the owner of the claim, had for many years been in the employ of the Hudson's Bay Company as master of one of their vessels trading on the coast, and having left their service and taken a claim at Chinook, was officiating as river pilot to the mail steamers from California." (Swann, 1857, 101)

James Scarborough, was from Scarborough Head, in Essex and sailed from England in September 1829 destined for Fort Vancouver. He was a second mate on the *Isabella* when the Hudson's

Bay Company ship arrived on the Columbia. After the loss of the *Isabella* on the bar, in the following year, 1830, he transferred to the *Llama*, and later served on the Company's famous steamer, the *Beaver*. He was the skipper of the *Cadboro* in 1838, and his last command was the schooner, *May Dacre*, Nathaniel Wyeth's ship, before he retired to his home in July 1850.

At the fort he met and married Ann Elizabeth, a Chinook Indian maiden and moved to the village of her father Chief Comcomly, on Baker's Bay, where they had four sons. He took a donation land claim of 648 acres, and built his home above Chinook Point. He established a thriving business exporting fish to England, and was paid in gold slugs, or ingots, accumulating a substantial sum of $60,000.

Captain Scarborough was known to keep quite a sum of money in his home at all times, and died very suddenly in February 1855. He instructed his servant, an elderly woman who lived with him, to take his money to the Hudson's Bay Co. at Chinook, or to people up the river. James Birnie of the HBCo., became the administrator of the Captain's estate, and Joe Brown, who worked for the Captain, found a sack containing $500, hanging from the rafters in the Captain's barn. Canvas bags holding ten to fifteen thousand dollars were found in the walls of his house. (Green, 1981, 27-28.)

The legend of Captain Scarborough's treasure says that he buried his gold somewhere on Chinook Hill. Gold ingots were reported to be buried in two sea chests, just a short distance from his home, but were never recovered. Then in the early nineteenth century, excavation for a new road which penetrated Scarborough Hill, revealed a wide variety of artifacts, including; stoneware, China bowls, brass chains and keys, boxes with brass tacks, thousands of beads, pocket knives, pistols, jewelry made of silver, and many trade articles. The most exciting discovery was gold. Sixty-seven pieces of gold and an additional quantity of other coins, spilled out after a bank caved-in during land clearing at Fort Columbia in 1903. News quickly spread through the community that Scarborough's treasure was actually found. Eight-sided fifty-dollar slugs were collected, the first documented discovery of the Captain's gold; along with English and Spanish coins dating back to 1773. (McDonald, 1966, 45-46.)

In 1864, the government purchased Chinook Point to build Fort Columbia, one of three fortifications installed near the mouth of the Columbia; the others being Fort Stevens and Fort Canby. Fort Columbia was maintained until the end of World War II and today it is a Washington State Park and Fort Columbia Museum. The museum mural was painted by Ernest Norling of Seattle, and includes the first white settlers, and the figure of Captain James Scarborough.

Captain Johnson

"In the fall of 1849 a party of Oregonians, embarked on a sailing vessel, and left California for Portland. The captain proved to be a most unkind and brutal master, not only to the sailors but to the passengers, who were compelled to eat the worst of food. After sailing for twenty-two days they encountered a violent gale, and were driven out of their course. As they were nearing the Columbia river bar the vessel was drawn into the breakers at North Beach and was deserted by captain , crew, and passengers, who in their haste to save themselves forgot their gold. On reaching shore they were exhausted and were obliged to walk around the entire night to keep from freezing. In the early morning they saw smoke a short distance up the beach. Each man hurried to the scene. They found a comfortable house where they were made to feel at home in true pioneer style by the owner, a Mr. Johnson, who was, as all Scotchmen are, loyal and hospitable. As they were in a weakened condition the good man gave them a small quantity of food at first, which was fish cooked on the point of a stick held before the fire. All agreed that was the best food they had ever eaten. Now they related their hardships encountered on the voyage. Mr. Johnson sent out his Indians with instructions to reach the wreck and bring everything available ashore. This order seemed scarcely possible, but the brave Indians went through the breakers, reaching the vessel, and before night brought all the sacks of gold dust and many articles of wearing apparel ashore, where each man could claim his own. The party remained several days with their benefactor, who kindly conveyed them to Astoria." (Cartwright, OHQ 1903, 62-63.)

Mr. Johnson

Captain James Johnson, a Scottish shipmaster, sailed around Cape Horn between 1840 and 1847 to the Catholic missions in California. In 1848, he arrived on the Columbia and was awarded a Donation Land claim of 640 acres, on Baker's Bay. The life of Captain Johnson has many amazing coincidences with that of Captain Scarborough, beginning with their first names. They were both ship captains, they held land claims near Baker's Bay, they married native women, they were both Columbia River pilots, and they buried gold on their property

The Scot was the salvage master of a shipwreck from the California mines, with a consignment of gold in its hold. During the salvage operations he removed part of the gold, (He removed part of the gold!) being crudely smelted slugs, valued at approximately $50 apiece.

In 1850, Captain Johnson built an eight-room house, with a massive fireplace, on the hill overlooking Baker's Bay, with a spectacular view of the Columbia River entrance. The English style home, was constructed with white pine from Maine, shipped around the Horn from New England.

Early one morning he observed with his spy-glass, two sailing ships, grounded on the beach, which had attempted to get over the bar, during the dark stormy night. He hurriedly gathered together his crew and rowed across the river to the wrecked ships. In one of the vessels he removed $20,000 in gold slugs, from the captain's cabin. The salvaged treasure was his, since there were apparently no survivors.

Ole Olson, a ship's carpenter, known as "the Swede," worked for Captain Johnson, and said that the captain showed him a few slugs taken from the wrecked ship's cabin.

Captain Johnson's neighbor and good friend, John Holman, who owned the only hotel in Pacific City, was invited over one morning, and was requested to bring along his gold scales. The captain then asked his visitor to wait while he made a trip to the back of his house and later returned with two heavy leather bags, filled with gold slugs. Mr. Holman weighed every slug, which came to a total of $20,000.

Gold Piece Spaded Up at Ilwaco

A $5 gold piece spaded up from the garden at the old W. B. Hawkins place at Ilwaco, by the new owner Charles Brandt in 1936, renewed interest in Captain Johnson's hidden treasure. Mr. Brandt, quickly made a down payment on the property after his fortunate discovery.

Captain Johnson wrapped his treasure in buckskin before displaying the gold slugs, as the '49ers called them, to two men shortly before he died in 1854. Don Whealdon, who grew up in Ilwaco, said "the captain had the money, he hid it, and up to date it has not been found." (Oregonian, March 30, 1936)

Robert Nash

The writer Robert Nash visited the site of Capt. Johnson's home, which was purchased in 1858, by Isaac Whealdon and his wife. There he saw the base of the old fireplace, the only visible remains of the home. In an article written for "Frontier Times," in 1967, he declared that the gold treasure was still buried. After doing some research, he was able to locate the whereabouts of a diary belonging to Mrs. Holman, who kept an accurate account of unusual events from the early 1800s. She verified the weighing of the gold slugs, by her husband and recorded other events which took place in those early years. The diary eventually passed to Mrs. J. Tobler.

The Whealdon's never claimed to have found the captain's hidden gold, and during the years they lived at Baker's Bay, they always hoped that one of the Johnson boys would return and recover their father's fortune. (Nash, 1967, 24-25.)

Oriental Junks
Wrecked Junks

The earliest history of China contains records of their ships sailing across the Pacific, known as the "eastern sea," in the ancient texts, to a land called Fu Sang. I learned of the early Chinese accounts of Fu Sang, from the author Henriette Mertz, who first wrote of her discovery in "Pale Ink." She searched the records of Chinese history for early seafarers who explored east to a land called Fu Sang, now thought to be America.

The surprising discovery of Chinese explorations to America, by Mertz, began with a book by Edward Vining, entitled, "An Inglorious Columbus," published in 1885. One of Vining's sources was an article from 1761, by M. De Guignes, who found the story in the Chinese classics. The original was retold by Ma Twan-lin, in his "Antiquarian Researches," from 1321.

The Asian adventurer, Hui Shen traveled in the fifth century, to a country east of China which Guignes, believed was Mexico. Hui Shen returned home in 429 A.D. and related the details of his journey to Yu-Kie, one of the princes of the court of the emperor, Wu-ti, in 502 A.D. The narrative was preserved in the Chinese historical account "Liang-See-Kong-Ki." In this record the country of Fu Sang was in the east, about 10,000 Li, or 3,000 miles east, which Henriette Mertz concludes was America, the southwestern portion, particularly, and Mexico.

The maps drawn in 1775 by Thomas Jefferys, Geographer to His Majesty George III, locates Fu Sang in the territory north of the entrance of Juan de Fuca. In his map this area is indicated as "Land which is supposed to be the Fu Sang of the Chinese Geographers."

In "Steel of Empire," the author John Murray Gibbon, said Hui Shen voyaged across the Pacific in the junk named *Tia Shan* about the end of the fifth century, and spent the winter at Nootka. In 1786, the crew from the *Nootka* commanded by John Meares, came across Chinese cash of the Tsin dynasty, 265-419 A.D., relics of the early Chinese visit.

1421

A Chinese junk was found buried under a sandbank in the Sacramento River, at the northern corner of San Francisco Bay, which Gavin Menzies learned, after giving a lecture to the Royal Geographic Society in London, in March 2002.

Dr. John Furry, of the Natural History Museum of Northern California, learned of the wreck after reading an account of some mysterious armor found in the hold of the ship. A magnetometer reading taken by Dr. Furry returned images of a buried ship 85 feet long and 30 feet wide, similar to trading junks of Zheng He's fleets. Samples of the wood were carbon-dated to 1410.

The remains of the teak ship at Nehalem were discussed in Menzies' book "1421, The Year China Discovered America." In this he mentions one of the old Nehalem wrecks and says that the ship's pulley was used for hoisting sails, made of calophyllum, native to Southeast Asia. He also said that Zheng He's ships used paraffin wax to desalinate seawater for the horses. (Menzies, 2002, 201-204)

Zheng He's fleets explored the world on nine voyages in the early fifteenth century.

One fleet included 300 ships. His ships were massive vessels, with a tremendous cargo capacity, some with nine masts, and four decks. One of the vessels was called a "Treasure Ship."

Old world travelers Marco Polo and Ibn Battuta, both described multi-masted Chinese ships, capable of carrying 500 to 1000 passengers.

S. A. Clarke

S. A. Clarke, *Pioneer Days of Oregon History*, 1900

S. A. Clarke recalled seeing the remains of two wrecks at the mouth of the Nehalem River in 1870; one he believed was a Chinese junk and the other was a ship of white survivors with heavy beards. This he learned from the Tillamook Indians in 1865. Mr. Clarke's book was written in 1900, and in chapter twenty-one, "Prehistoric Wrecks," he says that he kept a scrapbook which contained "several notices of treasure landed and buried on the beaches of Necarney that are various and curious. The Tillamook Indians told us, when we went there about thirty-five years ago their traditions of the past, one of which was concerning the Chinese junk wrecked on Nehalem sands; another was of a vessel from which white men with heavy beards were saved."

His family made a summer trip to Tillamook in 1870, and returned with pieces of beeswax. "My personal cognizance of it goes back to 1870, when my family made a summer trip from the Willamette to Tillamook, fifty or sixty miles south of the Columbia, and brought back small pieces of the beeswax, and also various traditions concerning the ancient wreck that might have left it there. The bones of two wrecks were then to be seen at the mouth of the Nehalem River, that enters the ocean a few miles north of Tillamook Bay.

Mr. Warren, who has been alluded to says his father heard from Swan, a very old Clatsop Indian, a story much the same that he had heard from his own father: That a long time ago a vessel was lost at Necarney Bay; that a number of her men came on shore, who carried a chest up the mountain and buried it on a bench; they carried up sacks full of treasure and poured into the chest, or placed the bags therein. Then the crew separated, some going north and some south.

As far back as earliest days of white men, in passing back and forth the Indians pointed out to them the mountain terrace where the treasure was supposed to be, but nothing could induce them to go near the spot.

Pirates, who waited and watched to capture the commerce of Spain, with the Orient, were not so very much out of the way in the latitude of Oregon. May it not have been possible that a mission ship had been captured by sea rovers, driven north, and was lost on this coast in that early time? If so, this vessel may have had on board supplies for the missions and churches of the entire coast.

Where the beeswax was found, at Nehalem Beach, there were also buried in the sand timbers fastened together by peculiar flat spikes, from half an inch to two inches wide and two to eight inches long. These were used in very hard woods, not like northern timber, and very durable – no doubt preserved by burial in the sands. These are in possession of Captain Edwards, examiner of hulls, at Portland, who wished some expert to identify them. It is thought they belonged to the wreck that carried the beeswax.

Not far south of Nehalem Beach is the Nestucca shore; at the southern extremity of this – as late as in 1882 – Major J. H. Turner, of Yamhill, saw timbers of a wreck cast up by the highest tides, that were very old; from these projected copper 'tree nails' an inch square. He had been a boat builder on Western waters and had knowledge of ship building. He thought the wood was white oak, and the construction indicated old age and old style. While he was there a very old Indian passed by to his fishing, and when asked what he knew of this wreck he said that his father told him it was there when he was young and long before his time, which would take it back for at least a century (approximately 1780).

Bancroft's "History of the Pacific States" gives a list of Chinese or Japanese wrecks that had been found for a century or more, either derelict on the seas or wrecked on the shores of North America. This confirms the legends of the coast Indians concerning the Oriental wreck that occurred at Nehalem, the bones of which, they assert, were to be seen in the sands at low tide in pioneer days. Such wrecks were also known along the shore north of the Columbia, or on the coast of Vancouver Island, as reported by those connected with the early time." (Clarke, 1900, 155-169)

In 1979, the trawler *Beaufort Sea* hauled in a large Asian urn, 15 nautical miles west of the entrance to the Strait of Juan de Fuca, from what is now known as the Asian Pot Wreck. Chinese storage jars have been caught by fisherman off the west coast of Vancouver Island, near Tofino and Pre-Columbian Chinese coins have also been found on the Island.

About the Author

Samuel Asahel Clarke was born in Cuba, the son of a plantation owner and educated in New York. He arrived in Oregon where he opened a sawmill in 1850, and then ventured south to the Umpqua gold rush in 1851. He took a land claim in 1852 near Salem, and a few years later was working in the city as a legislative clerk. He was the editor of the "Oregonian" during the last days of the Civil War, between 1864 and 1865. After the war, he was active in the Oregon and Californian Railroad Co., serving as a secretary for three years. He became the owner and editor of the *Salem Statesman*, and a part owner of the publication *Willamette Farmer*, 1867-1872. In 1878, he moved to Portland, where he became the head of the literary bureau of the Villard Railroad syndicate, until 1883. He was a librarian at the General Land Office, in Washington, D. C. between 1898 and 1908, and is the author of several works, tory.

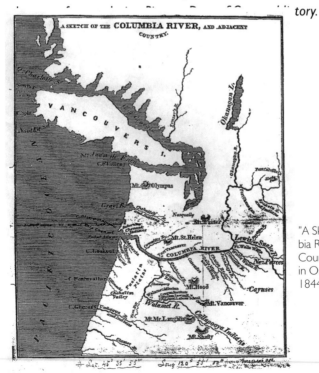

"A Sketch of the Columbia River, and Adjacent Country" from "Ten Years in Oregon" Lee & Frost, 1844.

Lee and Frost

After their missionary journeys through the northwest, Rev. Daniel Lee and Rev. Joseph H. Frost, recorded a short history of early Oregon, published in New York, in 1844, as *Ten Years in Oregon*. They saw the wrecked junk at Nehalem, several pieces of beeswax, and were recipients of Chinese pottery from the stranded Japanese junk near Cape Flattery. They also mentioned the travels of the famed botanist, David Douglas, who was staying at Fort Vancouver:

"The sand-bar at the mouth of the Columbia has been mentioned heretofore as being dangerous to those who are not well acquainted with the channel. In consequence of this obstruction, in the year 1828, the ship William and Ann was cast away a little within the bar…And on the 23^d of May, the ship Isabella was cast away upon a bar projecting from Sand Island opposite to Baker's Bay. As soon as she struck the men all deserted her, and without stopping at Fort George, made their way to Vancouver. It is thought that if they had remained on board until the tide served, she might have been saved; most of her cargo was saved. About thirty-or forty miles to the south of the Columbia are the remains of a vessel which was sunk in the sand near shore, probably from the coast of Asia, laden, at least in part, with bees-wax.(The Nehalem River is 35 miles south of the Columbia.) Great quantities of this wax have been purchased from the Killemook Indians by the Hudson's Bay Company and individuals; the writer also obtained a number of pounds of the same article from them while there, and was informed by them, that whenever the south-west storms prevail, it is driven on shore.

While living on the banks of the Columbia, an Indian girl who lived in the family brought in a piece one day which had drifted around with the tide, and lodged upon the beach of the river; this was as large as a man's fist…it was completely petrified. The writer presented it to Rev. Dr. Richmond when he left the country, in the autumn of 1842. And perhaps, it may not be considered out of place if I here state, that many of the streams of this country possess petrifying qualities, insomuch, that whole trees have been found in a state of perfect petrifaction. And the writer has now in his possession a piece of bark of the fir tree, which retains its natural appearance, but will, not withstanding, emit sparks when smitten with steel, like the flint.

In March, 1833, a Japanese junk was cast away fifteen miles to the south of Cape Flattery. Out of seventeen men, only three were saved. In the following May, Captain McNeil, of the Lama, brought the three survivors to Fort Vancouver; and from thence they were, in the following October, sent to England, to be forwarded to their own country.

From this wreck the writer has a beautiful China flower-pot, and a tea-cup, which were obtained from the Indians, having been in their possession since the time of the wreck. In the same year eleven Japanese in distress were drifted in a junk to Oahu, Sandwich Islands.

About this time a gentleman from Scotland, Mr. David Douglas, visited Oregon, under the patronage of the London Horticultural Society, for the purpose of scientific researches; and after fulfilling his mission returned to the Sandwich Islands, where he unfortunately lost his life.

The next party of American traders which crossed the Rocky Mountains after the abandonment of Astoria, was under the command of Captain Wyeth, in 1832. This is the same gentleman who headed the party across the mountains when the Messrs. J. and D. Lee and their associates came to the country as missionaries, under the patronage of the Missionary Society of the Methodist Episcopal Church, in 1834." (Lee and Frost, 1844, 106-109.)

The famous early naturalist, botanist, and scientist, David Douglas, made several trips to the Pacific Coast from England, between 1825 and 1833. He explored Saskatchewan, the Hudson Bay, British Columbia, the North Pacific Coast, California, Mexico and Hawaii. He established his headquarters at Fort Vancouver while exploring and studying the Oregon Country. He traveled through the Willamette Valley, down the Umpqua and McKenzie Rivers and then to the coast at present day Coos Bay.

He arrived on the *William & Ann* at Fort George on April 1, 1825. Dr McLoughlin journeyed downriver, by canoe, to meet the young botanist, soon after the brig's arrival. He was the Chief Factor's first guest at Fort Vancouver, sent by the Royal Horticultural Society of London, to study the Northwest Coast and collect specimens during his travels.

The *William & Ann,* a supply ship for the Hudson's Bay Co., was grounded on Clatsop Spit on March 11, 1829, and eventually lost.

Impressions and Observations of the Journal Man

"The finding of strange relics near the beach at Neah-kah-nie sets Mr. Lockley upon the track of Asiatic vessels known to have been thrown upon the Northwest coast of America well within the range of authentic history."

Mr. Lockley:

"While at Nehalem recently I went over to Neah-kah-nie Tavern to visit my old-time friend Sam Reed. We began talking of the old myths and traditions of buried treasure at the base of Neah-kah-nie, and he told me of a rather curious thing. He showed me two crudely-shaped bronze handles and an odd-shaped piece of metal, which he had found in a marshy place he was clearing for a garden.

Mr. Reed:

'There was a very large stump on the place said Mr. Reed. 'I directed the man who was helping me, to explode a few sticks of dynamite under it. The stump was blown clear out of the ground, leaving a hole as big as a cellar. In filling this hole and leveling it for the garden, we found these corroded old bronze handles, which had evidently, at some time, been under that huge stump I have no means of knowing whether the chest was buried there and the tree grew over it, or whether a hole was dug under the tree and the chest was buried there. I do not know. I do know, however, that the tree was several (hundred) years old, so that if the chest was buried there and the tree grew later, it goes to show there was travel up and down this coast at a very remote period.'

Oriental Junks

"There is no lack of myths and traditions of early-day ships having been lost on the Oregon coast. We have, however, records of not less than 15 Japanese vessels that have drifted ashore on the North Pacific coast during the past 100 years. The Japan warm stream, or, as the Japanese call it, the Kuro Siwo, sweeps in along the Pacific Northwest coast, moderating our climate and being the medium by which wrecked junks from Japan have drifted to this coast. Professor Davidson, in describing this great ocean river, says:

> The Northern equatorial current, leaving the coast of Lower California sweeps across the whole Pacific, with its axis two or three degrees south of the Sandwich Islands. Thence continuing on the parallel of 15 degrees, it sweeps northward until it passes the Ladrone, Islands, and is gradually deflected to the North and Northwest along the Asiatic coast in the parallel of 31 degrees. It washes the southern coast of Japan and passes along the northeastern coast of Nippon. Shortly thereafter the stream begins to spread and in latitude 38 degrees it splits into two streams. One branch, the Kamchatka current, moves to the northeast to Bering strait. The other follows the parallel of 35 degrees eastward. The main body of this branch comes directly toward the coast of America, is deflected southward and follows the west coast of Oregon and California, to be finally swept back into the great northern equatorial current. Japanese vessels that are disabled off the coast of Japan either drift with the Kamchatka current and are carried to the Aleutian islands, or missing these islands, they drift ashore along the Oregon and California coast.

In the fall of 1862 a Japanese vessel was wrecked on the island of Attu, in the Aleutian group. When dismantled this vessel had 12 men aboard. It drifted at the rate of 20 miles a day for 1800 miles, and when finally beached on the Aleutian islands only three of the crew were alive.

In 1871, the junk Jinko Maru of Matsaka, in the province of Ise, laden with rice, was wrecked on the island of Adakh, off Alaska.

This junk was dismasted on November 28, 1870, and drifted till May 5, 1871. Only a few members of the crew were alive after this long drift. They were taken by Captain Partridge, in command of the H. N. Hutchinson, to San Francisco and were returned from there to Japan. In 1848, Captain Cox picked up 20 Japanese from a disabled junk near the Alaskan coast.

In 1780, an employee of a Russian fur company rescued the crew of a Japanese junk that had drifted ashore on one of the Aleutian islands, and took them to Okhotsk and later to Irkutsk, where they stayed 10 years. In 1792, Empress Catherine sent these Japanese sailors aboard the ship Catherine to Hadodate, Japan. The Japanese refused to allow their fellow-countrymen to land.

About 124 years ago, a Japanese junk was wrecked on the coast near Sitka. The sailors lived on a small island just opposite Sitka, which was later named by the Russians, Japonski island. The compass of this junk passed into the possession of a surgeon in the United States Army. The shipwrecked crew of the junk built a craft and sailed for Japan, though whether they ever reached there is not known.

In 1813, a British brig named the Forester, en route from London to the mouth of the Columbia river under command of Captain John Jennings, discovered a Japanese junk of 700 tons burden abreast of Queen Charlottes' Island. The captain and two of the sailors had survived the 18 months' trip, living for most of this time on rainwater and beans.

In 1833, a Japanese junk came ashore near Cape Flattery. Most of the crew had died of starvation or scurvy. When the vessel came ashore the Indians boarded it and killed all of the surviving members of the crew except two men and a boy. One of these three survivors drew a picture of the junk ashore and of the Indians killing the crew and later bribed an Indian to give the drawing to some white man. The drawing came into the possession of the Hudson's Bay officials and Captain McNeil was dispatched to Cape Flattery to investigate. He bought these three Japanese from the natives and they were forwarded to England. From there they were sent aboard the Morrison, under command of C. W. King, to Japan. The Japanese refused to allow them to be landed in the Bay of Yeddo, and they were taken to Kagoshima. The Japanese refused to allow them to be landed there, and fired at the boat; so they were taken to Macao. Porcelainware from this Japanese junk was for years afterward found among the Indians in the vicinity of Cape Flattery.

Years before the coming of the whites a Japanese junk was wrecked on Point Adams, south of the mouth of the Columbia river. Sir Edward Belcher, who was at Astoria in 1839, inquired of the Indians about this wreck. The Indians told him the vessel was broken up by the surf on Clatsop Beach, that her crew landed safe on shore, and that when the boat broke up a large amount of beeswax was thrown up on the beach. Professor Davidson in 1851 secured a considerable quantity of this wax.

On the 24th of March, 1815, the brig Forrester, while off the coast of California went to the rescue of a Japanese junk that was in distress. This junk had lost its mast and rudder. It came from the port of Osaka, in Japan. Most of the crew of 35 men had died during the 17 months that the junk had been drifting. It had traveled about 5300 miles during its 516 days of drifting.

These are but a few of the many Japanese vessels that have been carried by the Japanese current to the shores of Oregon, Washington or Alaska. Whether Japanese junks drifted ashore centuries ago, along the Oregon and Washington coast, is not known, but it is not at all improbable." (Lockley, Oregon Journal 1924)

Notes:

The Japanese junk scattered beeswax along the shore, as described by Bancroft: "a junk laden with wax was thrown upon Point Adams in 1820."

Fifteen Japanese vessels have drifted ashore on the North Pacific coast during the past 100 years.

Captain Jennings came upon a Japanese junk of 700 tons at Queen Charlottes Island in 1813 and again two years later off the California coast another Japanese junk from Osaka, that lost its mast and rudder.

Pacific Flotsam

Oceanographers have followed cargo spills of container ships to better understand ocean currents. Somewhere along a freighters Pacific route, five containers of Nike shoes washed overboard in a storm in 1990. Six months later they began to arrive on the Northwest coast. Due to the curvature of the shoes, the left-footed ones came to Oregon and the right-footed shoes landed further north, on Washington shores.

A native Alaskan provided a new house for his family after a prefabricated home came ashore in a crate. In Northwest Washington a load of wood siding was also a coastal arrival, which provided housing for a couple who had recently moved there. (Moody, 2006, "Nike Flotsam" 142-147)

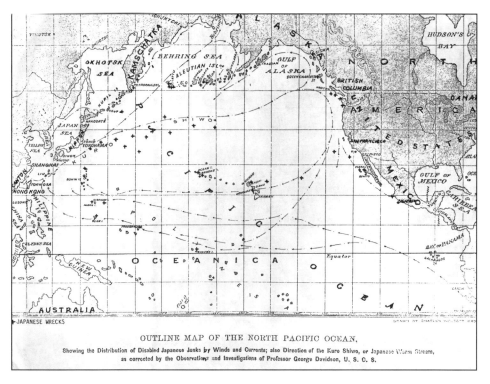

"Outline Map of the North Pacific Ocean, Showing the Distribution of Disabled Japanese Junks by Winds and Currents; also Direction of the Kuro Shiwo, or Japanese Warm Stream, as corrected by the Observations and Investigations of Professor George Davidson, U. S. C. S." 1876.

Oriental Junks

Brooks and Davis

On their journey along the Oregon coast in 1848, Solomon Smith and John Hobson reported that there were "several pieces of a junk, between Clatsop and Nehalem." Hobson believed they were Chinese, which were known to have carried beeswax, but not in the great quantities as the Spanish galleons.

The earliest recordings of Oriental junks to the Pacific Coast, can be attributed to Charles Wolcott Brooks and Horace Davis. Brooks was working for the Japanese government at the port of San Francisco, between 1853 and 1875. One of his reports, published by the California Academy of Sciences in 1876, provides details on sixty ships, the survivors, cargo, and events encountered between 1613 and 1876; entitled *Japanese Wrecks, Stranded and Picked up Adrift in the North Pacific Ocean.*

Horace Davis read his paper before the American Antiquarian Society in April 1872, and published the same year, in Worcester, Massachusetts as, *Record of Japanese Vessels Driven Upon the North-West Coast of America and its Outlying Islands.* He begins with the sighting of Captain C. M. Scammon, of the U. S. Rev. Marine, who discovered a wreck, which was reported in the *Daily Alta California,* April 22, 1860:

> In 1853 there was found on the southwest and largest of the San Benito Group, the remains of what was supposed to be a Japanese junk; whether it was some part of those said to have been cast away on the coast of Oregon several years ago, or the relic of some other eastern sailing craft, is a subject of conjecture. That it was one or the other there can be no doubt. The planks were fastened together on the edges with spikes or bolts of a flat shape, with the head all on one side. The seams were not straight, although the workmanship was otherwise good. It appeared to be the bottom of a vessel that was seen here and gave evidence of having been a long time on shore.

(Mr. Clarke's description of a Chinese junk, with "timbers fastened together by peculiar flat spikes" sounds like the type of junk that Mr. Scammon saw in 1853, a Japanese junk, and the wreckage which came ashore at Arch Cape in 1894.)

Mr. Davis then goes on to the wreck at Point Adams, which occurred sometime between 1810 and 1820, and tells us that his source for this record came from Capt. Edward Belcher, who was living in Astoria in 1839:

> A wreck likewise occurred in this bay, many years ago. It appears that a vessel with many hands on board, and laden with bees-wax, entered the bay and was wrecked, she went to pieces, and the crew got on shore. Many articles were washed on shore, and particularly the bees-wax. This latter is even now occasionally thrown upon the beach, but in smaller quantities than formerly. I have one specimen now in my possession.

Mr. Davis then reports on the work of Prof. Davidson, from his "Coast Pilot of California, Oregon and Washington Territory," U. S. Coast Survey, 1869. "There are occasionally, after great storms, pieces of this wax thrown ashore, coated with sand and bleached nearly white. Formerly a great deal was found, but now it is rarely met with. Many people on the Columbia possess specimens, and we have seen several pieces."

Professor George Davidson was in charge of the U. S. Coast Survey on the Pacific, and was stationed at the mouth of the Columbia River in 1851, where he conducted his investigations.

James Swann mentions the Japanese junk, wrecked near Cape Flattery, and the three sailors in his book "The Northwest Coast," from 1857. He also includes another Asian junk, with a cargo of beeswax:

> There is also a tradition among the Indians that a Chinese or Japanese junk was wrecked years ago on Clatsop Beach, south of the Columbia. Part of her cargo was beeswax. And to prove the correctness of this tradition, there are to this day occasionally, after great storms, lumps and pieces of this wax found on the beach…I have had some of this wax given me by an old

Indian doctor...The specimen was sent by me to the California Academy of Natural Sciences. Wilkes also mentions the fact of a Chinese junk having been wrecked at Point Grenville in 1833, and three of the Japanese were rescued from the Indians by the Hudson Bay Company. (Swann, 1857, 206)

Lieutenant Charles Wilkes, of the U. S. Exploring Expedition, said the officers of the Hudson's Bay Company were made aware of the Japanese junk's disaster, when they received a drawing on a piece of China-paper, illustrating three shipwrecked sailors, with the junk on the rocks, and the Indians in the act of plundering. Captain McNeal rescued the three crewmen from slavery, who turned out to be, two men and a boy, and he said that there was some trouble in purchasing the boy. When the *Eagle* sailed for London in the fall, with the annual cargo of furs, the Japanese sailors were aboard, and finally were returned to their home in 1837. (Bancroft, 1884, 533 and Wilkes, iv. 315-316)

An article of porcelain was given to Mr. Birnie, the agent of the HBC, as a memorial of the event.

The name of the Japanese survivors' vessel was the *Hojun-maru,* which left the port of Nagoya in October 1832, with a cargo of rice, and other gifts for the annual tribute to the Shogun. The voyage would have only been about 400 miles to Tokyo, but the junk was caught in a typhoon – her rudder snapped, and the mast sail became useless. They were swept by the Kuro shiwo current, east, and the ship drifted for months. The original fourteen man crew survived on rice and rainwater, until only three remained.

After fourteen months adrift, the vessel finally washed ashore near Cape Flattery. The three seamen who survived were: Otokichi, Kyukichi, and Iwakichi. They lasted the first winter as slaves of the Makah Indians, who traded with the HBC, where the news of their captivity reached Dr McLoughlin. Captain William McNeil, of the *Llama,* rescued the castaways, and returned to Fort Vancouver.

Ranald MacDonald met the three Japanese sailors when he was a child. He was born at Fort Astoria to Archibald McDonald, a Scotsman, working for the HBC as a fur-trader, and Raven, also known as Princess Sunday, a Chinook Indian, and daughter of the famous

Chief Comcomly. His Indian relatives told him that their ancestors had come from Asia. He then developed a fascination to learn more about Japan. Following the wishes of his father, he was educated at the Red River Academy, in Manitoba, Canada, and later gained a position as a bank clerk. He signed on the whaling ship *Plymouth* in 1845, and convinced the captain to set him free in a small boat off the coast of Hokkaido. On July 1, he went ashore on the island of Rishiri, and was soon captured by the Ainu residents. He was then sent to Nagasaki, where he was confined for ten months, during which time he studied the Japanese language. He was taken aboard the American warship USS *Preble*, under Captain James Glynn in April 1849, along with fifteen other castaways, and returned to North America.

He was the first man to teach the English language in Japan and was also the instructor of Einosuke Moriyama, one of the interpreters during the negotiations between Commodore Perry and the Japanese representative, the Tokugawa Shogunate.

Archaeology

Archaeological excavations at Fort Vancouver began in 1947. All traces of the fort vanished before efforts were made to mark its exact location, but seekers were aided by archives and archaeology. Fort Vancouver was the headquarters for the Hudson's Bay Company Columbia Department. The British company moved their operations from Fort George at Astoria, to the Vancouver site in 1825, one hundred miles upriver.

The fort's palisade constructed of 15 foot fir posts, surrounded an area 734 feet by 318 feet and enclosed more than a dozen structures, including; the Chief Factor's residence of Dr. John McLoughlin, a kitchen, wash house, bake house, blacksmith shop, carpenter shop, the fur warehouse, and the trade shop and dispensary.

The fort Vancouver National Historic site currently curates over 2 million artifacts, with almost 200,000 in the study collection. The Fort Vancouver Visitors Center and Museum displays many of the artifacts recovered during the excavations.

Hudson's Bay Company brass trade tokens.

Northwest Company tokens were made of brass and copper.

Chamber pot from the U. S. Exploring Expedition 1838-1842, commanded by Lt. Charles Wilkes.

Blue and white Ming Dynasty porcelain dinnerware, known as "Cantonware" carried by Spanish, English, American and Asian vessels.

Chinese "Ginger jar" used for transporting various foods and storage.

Fort Vancouver drawing by Gustavus Sohon 1855. The Hudson's Bay Company fort on the right and at the top of the hill, left, Vancouver Barracks, U. S. Army.

This coin was worn as a necklace,
a half-dime, ca. early 1800s.

Kanaka village.

Collection of Spode ceramics.

Illustration by Richard Schlecht is a recreation of what the fort may have looked like in 1845.

"What may represent an historic momento of the famous round-the-world United States Exploring Expedition of 1838-1842 was a broken chamber from Trash Pit no. 4. this ceramic gem had the United States Navy coat of arms with the wording, ""Come Box the Compass" and "May Success Attend Our Agriculture, Trade, and Manufactures." Could this item which may have traveled almost around the world have belonged to Lieut. George Foster Emmons, U. S. Navy, who, after the wreck of the sloop-of-war Peacock at the mouth of the Columbia River in 1841, stayed at Fort Vancouver as the guest of Dr John McLoughlin? Fortunately, or unfortunately, some Indian maiden may have carelessly dropped this chamber and left for posterity the fact that Lieutenant Emmons had slept at Fort Vancouver.

The finding of some Chinese porcelain and other wares of probable Chinese manufacture follows in line with the excavations at Fort Spokane, Fort Okanogan and Fort Walla Walla. Ceramics of Chinese manufacture are fairly well documented. Commercial relations between the Philippines and New Spain were well established before 1600. Trading galleons were making regular runs between Luzon and the west coast of Mexico carrying among other things quantities of Chinese porcelains and crockery storage jars filled with products of the Far East. Evidence of this intercourse is found wherever Spain's colonial system left its mark. In the ruins of the missions and presidios from Florida to California such evidence is common. Even Drake as he coasted northward in 1579 took as prizes a number of Spanish ships and transferred to his own vessels crates of Chinese porcelains, fragments of which apparently have been found around Drakes Bay in northern California. Cermeno, coming sixteen years later from Manila bound for Acapulco, unfortunately was shipwrecked in this same bay and left additional Chinese ceramics which were widely distributed by the local Indians to their numerous villages.

In later years, after the decline of Spanish world supremacy, we find that Chinese products continued to find their way to the west coast of the New World in English and American vessels. Exactly how porcelains and crockery found their way to the Hudson's Bay

Company posts is not known but the evidence was uncovered during the excavations, not in large quantities as compared to the English wares but in sufficient amounts for the purpose of study. Fragments were found to determine that the shapes included bowls, plates, cups and ginger jars in the white porcelain decorated with blue and black line designs." (Caywood, 1955, 56-57)

Items of trade used by the Lewis & Clark Expedition, the Pacific Fur Company, the Northwest Company, and the Hudson's Bay Company, included blue beads, buttons, and coins, which were found in the various Tillamook Indian villages. One of these was known as Chisucks, on the Wilson River. Lewis & Clark sketched this village in 1806, at Elk Creek, on their Tillamook Bay map. There were over 400 glass trade beads found here and two brass trade buttons, a brass trade pipe, two fragments of China and one Chinese coin, dated 1820. (S. A. Clarke said that bearded white sailors used copper Chinese coins, with square holes to trade for furs, and fired guns to signal their arrival.) The origin of the Chinese coins was most likely Canton, a major sea-otter fur-trading city. The most astonishing piece excavated was a chunk of beeswax about six inches wide, eight inches long, and four inches deep.

Many other pieces of beeswax have been picked up at other village sites, such as Nat-Ti on Nehalem Bay, Kil-Har-Nar on Tillamook Bay and the site on Bay Ocean sand spit. There were six pieces of iron uncovered at the Netarts site, and fragments of china from the Chien Lung Dynasty, dated to 1790.

Chinese coins have been discovered near Cape Flattery, at the mouth of the Columbia River, and other sites along the Oregon coast. An archaeological site near the Trojan Nuclear facility yielded three coins during excavations between 1969 and 1971. Two of the coins were from the K'ang-Hsi period, about 1662-1725.

They have also been found near the Bonneville Dam, the Chief Joseph Dam in Washington, in the Scappoose area, near Carver and Gladstone.

An article in the "Smithsonian" entitled "Chinese Relics in Alaska" from 1892, written by Lt. T. Dix Bolles, of the U. S. Navy, described a wooden mask that was donated to the museum in the 1880's. The native creation was removed from a grave near Chilcat Village, and found with two large bronze Chinese coins, that were used for eyes. The local Chilcats said the grave was that of a medicine man, who died two hundred years earlier, which dates the mask to the late 1600's, and the coins were believed to have arrived on a Chinese junk.

Dan Lawrence of Tillamook, picked up an old Chinese coin on the beach in 1955, that had a triangular hole in the center. A report from the editor of "Numismatic Review" determined that the coin was from the reign of Emperor Chien Lung, 1736-1796. His mother also received a newspaper clipping that reported the discovery of a bronze Chinese coin unearthed four miles south of Junction City, Oregon, and surprisingly was from the same period of Chien Lung.

A Chinese coin was recently discovered near Depoe Bay, dated to between 1420 and 1430.

Netarts sand spit, site of a late prehistoric village. (author photo)

Tillamook Excavations

Archaeological excavations were made by the field crew of Portland State University, between 1956 and 1959, under Dr. Thomas Newman. At the "Tillamook Site" the students removed a surprising number of artifacts: "Decomposed iron fragments, a copper pendant, and nearly 100 sherds of Chinese porcelain." The age of the site and the artifacts showed "that the prehistoric occupation continued into the era of Euro-American trade, which was well begun along the coast by the 1790s."

"A sophisticated restudy of the Chinese porcelains from Tillamook has shed interesting new light on their implications. Several lines of technical evidence suggest that the porcelains were of Chinese Ming or Ch'ing (Qing) Dynasty manufacture, made sometime between AD 1573 and 1722. This is well before the era of intensive Euro-American trade along the Oregon Coast, and the authors suggest that the specimens might actually have been salvaged by the Tillamook people from the wreckage of an early European merchant vessel. A likely candidate would be one of the Spanish galleons on the regular Acapulco-Manila run, which was made annually across the Pacific for 250 years, from 1565 to 1815. The route of the Manila Galleon passed along the Northwest Coast, and the San Antonio, lost in 1604, or the San Francisco Xavier, lost in either 1705 or 1707, (accounts differ) with 'a quantity of porcelain' on board, are two possible sources of the Tillamook porcelains (Beals and Steele 1981)."

"Large blocks and candles of beeswax, found in amazing quantity along the Tillamook shore, are further evidence of late prehistoric/early historic shipwrecks. As summarized by Woodward (1986), large quantities of beeswax from the north coast of Oregon were documented as early as 1813. One 1908 report estimated the quantity found there at about twelve tons, and said that some six tons had been shipped to Hawaii around 1847. Woodward also describes other finds of Chinese porcelains from the coast, including flaked projectile points and other tools made by local natives from porcelain fragments." Two Carbon 14 dates on a sample of the wax placed it in the same general time range as the porcelains.

"Possible sources of these exotic materials, other than the Manila Galleons, could have been Japanese or Portuguese trading vessels disabled in typhoons along the Asian shore, and carried to the west coast of North America by the Japanese Current. Many examples of such inadvertent drift voyages are documented for the 19th century. Continuing research may be expected to further illuminate this earliest Oregon contact with Old World cultures."

At "Fishing Rocks," at the mouth of the Columbia River, on the Washington side, the archaeologists again uncovered Chinese porcelain; "fragments of Chinese porcelain, chimney glass and metal." The site showed evidence of repeated use as a fishing and hunting camp. (Aikens, 1993, 165-170, also Beals, "Chinese porcelains – 1981)

Another important Indian village was excavated near Seaside, called the Primrose site, one of several along the south Clatsop plain, and is also one of the rare shell middens on the Oregon coast. Here there is a large rectangular house, which appeared to have been built and rebuilt several times, according to the authors Kenneth Ames and Herbert Maschner, between 350 BC and 400 AD.

Speaking of early European contact with Northwest Coast Indians, in "Peoples of the Northwest Coast" the authors stated that metal objects had been recovered from sites along the coast, which included Ozette, at the northwest tip of Washington, just south of Cape Flattery, and Cathlapotle, on the Columbia, near Portland. The source of the metal was Asia, either from trade, or from Oriental vessels, which crossed the Pacific. (Ames and Maschner, 1999, 266)

Note: When Mr. Clarke's family made a summer trip to Tillamook in 1870 they returned with pieces of beeswax and traditions of the ancient wreck from the Indians. There he saw the bones of two wrecks at the mouth of the Nehalem River.

Alison Stenger, of The Oregon Archaeological Society, believes that the porcelain from Nehalem and Netarts, represents two different cargos, suggesting two wrecks from the East. One of these she refers to as the "Chinaman Wreck," exposed in 1901, and located at the southern end of the Nehalem spit. A journal describing the location of the ship with a map and illustrations of porcelain fragments, was sent to her by a member of the Nehalem Bay Historical Society.

The shipwreck that is believed to be Spanish is located near the "Witness Tree" a large blue spruce north of the Nehalem sand spit, and close to the road that connects Manzanita with the Nehalem peninsula. The wreck was revealed after storms and was "partially excavated by a group from Astoria."

I he time period for the prehistoric sites, the teak and the porcelain shards, that were uncovered, are closely related. (Stenger, "Screenings" 2005)

The Dalles-Deschutes Excavations

An archaeological team from the University of California, Berkeley, worked the Indian burial sites along the Columbia River, in the 1920s, and printed the report of their excavations in *Archaeology of The Dalles-Deschutes Region*, 1930. The work of the science team provided a glimpse of the articles that were traded by the earliest pioneers:

Phoenix buttons "have been reported from Indian graves near Astoria at the mouth of the Columbia. They are present in several Portland museums, in the DeYoung Memorial Museum, San Francisco, in the American Museum of Natural History, New York, and doubtless in a number of other places that have not happened to come to our notice. Schenck even picked up a small size, no. 8, amid the ruins of the old Spanish mission at Santo Domingo, Baja California, Mexico. Yet such a definite, clear cut, suggestive device so widely distributed and apparently existing in large numbers has not been identified, so far as we have been able to determine, by any of these institutions. It makes the tracing of relationships of simple bone and stone artifacts look rather hopeless. No doubt the buttons originated with some of the early traders on the coast and their occurrence as far south as Baja California suggests the sea-otter hunters who carried their operations from Alaska that far south. There was a ship "Phoenix," Captain Hugh Moor (or Moore), from

Bengal that traded at least along the Alaskan and British Columbian coasts from 1792-95. During this time Baranof, subsequently head of the American operations of the Russian American Company, became more than ordinarily friendly with her captain, and when Baranof launched his company's ship he called her the "Phoenix." This "Phoenix" served as the company's official means of communication between Alaska and Okhotsk until wrecked in 1800. The Russian American Company's activities were such as to make the observed Phoenix button distribution probable and there is this faint connection between that company and the Phoenix idea. Neither the Hudson's Bay Company nor the Northwest Company nor any of the other established trading companies seem to have had any connection with a Phoenix motif.

A probable origin is suggested by Mr. Howland Wood of the American Numismatic Society. He believes that the buttons were undoubtedly made in New England about 1828 for the Greek patriots fighting for independence from the Turks. Some of them may be assumed to have remained in the hands of the makers and to have thus become part of the trading supplies of some of the New England sea-captains trading on the Pacific coast."

"Since the above was written, Mr. C. L. Marshall, of Portland, Oregon has brought to our notice an excellent article on these buttons by C. Corbly Church, which appeared in The Sunday Oregonian of August 12, 1928. Church presents a good case for the making of the buttons for Christophe, Haiti about 1812." (Strong, Schenck and Steward, 1930, 64-65)

Voyage of the East Indiaman *Phoenix*

In Howay's, 1930 publication, "List of trading vessels in the maritime Fur Trade, 1785-1794," he indicates the presence of the *Phoenix*, on the Northwest coast, a British barque from Bengal, commanded by Hugh Moore, in 1792.

Alexander Baranov, Chief Manager of the Russian American Company, saw the ship in the Chugach Gulf or Prince William Sound, in May 1792, listed in a letter he wrote on July 24th 1793:

I saw there an English ship, which was from East India, was in Canton, in Manila, and in America, stopping near Nootka. It followed along the shore to Chugach, trading with different natives, and gathered many furs. On the way, in a storm it was dismasted and in Chugach was repaired. She was named the *Phoenix* and from here intended to return direct to Canton.

Baranov constructed a ship on the coast of Alaska in 1794 and christened it after the East Indiaman *Phoenix*, that was sadly lost with all hands in 1799, on a return trip from Okhotsk.(Andrews, 1932, 35)

Clackamas Indian Grave Yields Trader's Wares

Youths who were fishing on the Clackamas River accidentally pushed one of their poles into a hidden Indian grave, containing "bracelets, and anklets of copper, stringed beads, and silver. Necklaces of wampum, discs of copper punched for stringing, keys, thimbles, and buttons." The hidden cache also revealed one Chinese coin, dated to between 1736 and 1796, during the reign of Emperor Chien Lung.

"It is a far cry, indeed, from palm-fringed Haiti to the alder-lined banks of the Clackamas river. And from the beginning of the 19th century to the present day. But the gap has been bridged in a most unusual manner," says Oregonian writer, C. Corbly Church. "Bits of metal, green with the corrosion of years, strung with wampum, bright colored beads and fragments of glass were among the treasures unearthed recently near Gladstone, Or. When burnished, these buttons, for such they were, disclosed the wide-spread wings and swan-like neck of a phoenix arising from a bed of flames, and the inscription: "Je renais de mes cendres."

"The unusual representation of the phoenix" was so rare that a search of museums of the world revealed only one representation of the bird stamped on the copper, silver and gold coins struck with the image of King Christophe, of Haiti, on the obverse side in the year 1820.

Two clues or leads became evident. "In the first place, the date of the buttons' manufacture was estimated by the buttonists to have been within the period 1795 to 1830." The second piece of evidence. "Came through the finding of a shako plate dated about 1805 which bears a crown identical with the crown of the phoenix but on the head of an imperial eagle. This shako plate was at one time worn by an imperial guard of Jacques Dessalines, first emperor of Haiti."

"Coins issued by Christophe in the years 1812 to 1820 bear both his bust and this coat-of-arms. The phoenix on one of these coins in the possession of the numismatic department of the United Sates Mint, in comparison with the phoenix on the button, is the outstanding argument for the belief in the Haitian origin of the latter."

If the buttons were made for the Haitian army, how did they find their way to the Clackamas Indian grave? "The Clackamas Indian acted as host to the trader Indians who met at the falls to exchange cayuses and dried salmon for the blankets, vermillion, turquoise and trinkets which the Spaniards furnished the Indian trade in the south. Chief among the travelers who descended the Clackamas from its headwaters and from the skyline trade route which extended south along the ridge of the Cascades, were the Molallas, or Waiilatpuans, who were identical with the Waiilatpuanso or Cayuse Indians of Wasco, Morrow and Union counties." (Church, Oregonian, 1928)

The other sources for the buttons could have been the traders of Astor's Pacific Fur Company, the Northwest Company, or the Hudson's Bay Company.

Phoenix buttons were found in great numbers along the Columbia River and in the Tillamook country. In addition to The Dalles – Deschutes sites, they were uncovered in Tillamook, and at Sauvies Island, on the Willamette River, just west of Portland. The buttons could have been carried by Nathaniel Wyeth, who established Fort William on the Island in 1832. The old Wilson River trade routes ended in that area, and the Island site was abandoned in 1835.

Before arriving in the Northwest, Nathaniel Wyeth took a shipload of ice from Boston to Haiti. "It could well be that he found out about the supply of 'Phoenix' buttons there and realized their value as trade items in his project in the Northwest. Coincidently, many of those buttons, along with some marked "A J Tower & Co. Boston," have been found along the south shore of Sauvies Island near where Wyeth established Fort William." (Caywood, 1955, 48)

"Pair of Carved Stone Heads Revives Indian Tradition – Archaeological Find on the Lower Columbia Recalls Story of Shipwreck at River's Mouth at Early Day," *Oregon Journal,* **November 24, 1912.**

"At Samuel Hill's place at Maryhill on the Columbia river recently there was found a pair of remarkable stone heads, which seem likely to prove one more of the many unanswered archaeological questions. Mr. Hill mentioned them to Edward S. Curtis, and suggested that he visit Maryhill and see what he thought of them. Mr. Curtis made a series of pictures showing all lines of the heads, and will submit copies of them to the leading archaeologists of this country and Europe, in order to learn if there is anything comparable to any museum, and also to get the opinions of different scientists as to what they are and who made them.

The natural supposition is that they were carved by prehistoric Indians. This is borne out by the fact that they were unearthed on the site of an old Indian village, and near a remarkable Indian burying ground, and carved from stone native to the locality. To dispute such a theory is the fact that the features are not Indian; and yet the carving seems to be that of Indian hands. Mr. Curtis suggests a thought as to the origin, but insists that it is only a theory , and one naturally occurring to a person particularly well versed in the traditions of Columbia river tribes. To quote his words: 'There is a tradition of a shipwreck at the mouth of the Columbia. Several survivors (some say four, others two) reached shore, where the daughter of the Clatsop chief found them, and in the usual dramatic way of traditions succeeded in saving their lives. She married the leader of the party, whom the Indians call Kunupi (probably a corruption of a Spanish name). This tradition is so clear that the actions of the men, their personal appearance and the character of the wreckage are definitely described. According to the legend, they were all bearded men, and as they were first discovered in the act of popping corn on the beach, it is to be assumed that the vessel was from Mexico and the sailors were Spanish.

They remained at the mouth of the Columbia a few years, building their house in a place which became known as Kunupi, as it is still called by the native survivors of the region. Then they went up the river, presumably in an effort to reach the Atlantic coast by an overland journey.

Thus far the tradition is recited by the two sole survivors of the Chinook, sisters who claim descent from Kunupi. Just at this point the story of an old Cascade woman seems to fit in perfectly. Two bearded white men, she says, suddenly appeared in the populous villages at the Cascades of the Columbia. Because of the ornamental bits of brass which one of them, whom she calls Soto (another Spanish name manufactured), the Indians received them kindly, gave them lodging, food and wives. There the white men lived for some years, when they departed eastward, and no further trace of them exists in history or in Indian tradition. No doubt they were killed by the Snakes or other mountain tribes, who were at all times hostile to the river tribes. The narrator of this tradition exhibits some of the brass ornaments made by Soto and inherited from her father, the Cascade chief, who was hanged in the war of 1856.

That these traditions are authentic there can be no doubt. Alexander Henry in 1813 was surprised to meet at the mouth of the Columbia 'a man about 30 years of age, who has extraordinarily dark red hair, and is the supposed offspring of a ship that was wrecked within a few miles of the entrance of this river many years ago.' Again, in 1811, Franchere met at the Cascades an old man who said that he was the son of a Spaniard, one of four survivors of a wreck at the mouth of the Columbia. These unknown Spaniards were probably the first white men to behold the Columbia.

Now to return to the two sculptured heads. They were found within about 80 miles of the place where Soto, and after him his half-breed son, lived in the Cascade village, and it does not seem impossible that some Indian artist carved them in an effort to depict the strange visitors. Indian priests were apt to fashion from wood, bone or stone figures representing creatures whom they associated with the supernatural. These white men were strange in appearance and could do many things inexplicable to the native. Associating them with the supernatural, it would be perfectly natural for an Indian to carve these heads and consider them a part of his collection of sacred objects, through which he would expect to receive from supernatural sources assistance and strength and perhaps some of the powers of these strange men. As the heads have every indication of being old of Indian workmanship, and yet representing the Caucasian type, the above theory seems worthy of consideration.'

"Not far from the above spot some strange carvings have been found by Captain Winslow of the United States survey, which depict the chase of a deer, a turtle, a snake and warriors and nearby are frequently found many arrow heads of quaint workmanship."

Marine Archaeology

Siletz Bay Mystery Ship

The maritime writer, Stan Allyn, tells the story of a mystery ship that sailed into Siletz Bay, sometime in the dim past, and ran aground, leaving no survivors. The legend was passed down for generations, of this shipwreck, which carried a cargo of sacked meal, dumped by the native Americans, in favor of the sacks. The tale is from the "Pioneer History of North Lincoln County, Oregon" by Earl Nelson.

An unidentified shipwreck was uncovered, in 1972, at low tide, on the east shore of Siletz Bay, just southwest of the mouth of Schooner Creek. Some marine historians believe it could be the *Sunbeam*, a 100 foot schooner which left the Golden Gate, of San Francisco, in the late 1880s and was never heard from again. Another chronicler says that it could be the *Uncle John*, a 113 ton schooner lost off Cape Foulweather, in March, 1876, and another possibility, is the schooner *Phoebe Fay*, stranded off the rough Foulweather Cape again, in April, 1882.

Oriental Junks

The actual identity of this unknown vessel remains a mystery, but it could be the lost schooner, *Blanco*, which was built at North Bend, for A. M. Simpson in 1860, and reportedly capsized off the Siletz in 1864, and drifted into the bay. The ship was underway from San Francisco, on November 16, 1864, with Captain Kelcher in command, and what actually happened after it set a course for Coos Bay is unknown. The battered hull eventually drifted into the bay and washed ashore near a creek, now called Schooner, after the shipwreck. There were no signs of her crew and they were never found.

A letter written by Ben Simpson, the Indian agent for the Siletz Indian Agency, in 1864 to H. H. Luce of Coos Bay, sheds some light on the fate of the *Blanco*: "A large brig named *Blanco* from San Francisco was wrecked a few days since at the mouth of Siletz River. I have just returned from an examination of the vessel. She is a total wreck – her masts are gone her deck broken in, her hull split from deck to keel, and I fear her crew are all lost. I found some iron, both round and flat, still in her hull, and also I found a small lot of rope rigging. In addition to this I found some articles in possession of the Indians." (Allyn, Oregonian, 1972)

Twenty Dollar Gold Pieces

Eleanor Johns, a young Siletz Indian girl, picked up an old canvas belt in a garbage dump, just north of Siletz, in 1939, which held 26 twenty dollar gold pieces. She ran home to show her mother her discovery, not knowing what the bright shiny objects were. The next morning she was taken to the district attorney, who arranged for the state police to investigate her discovery. The investigators were unable to locate the owner of the treasure, who may have been an old Siletz Indian, so the gold coins were placed in a bank vault for Eleanor. Six of the coins disappeared sometime before authorities took charge of the investigation. The dates of the coins ranged from the earliest days of settlement to the most recent minting. (Oregon Journal, 1939)

Sunshine

In *Lewis & Dryden's Marine History of the Pacific Northwest*, the mystery of the schooner *Sunshine* and the fate of its crew was reported in 1895: "In November a mysterious fate over took the crew of the schooner *Sunshine*, built at Coos Bay in September, 1875. In command of Capt. George Bennett, who was also half owner of the vessel, she arrived at San Francisco on her first trip October 8th, and, after discharging her lumber cargo, sailed fore her home port after leaving the Bay City until November 18th, when her hull was seen floating bottom up close in shore north of Cape Hancock, and a few days later it drifted ashore near Easterbrook's place, Long Beach, so badly wrecked that no clew could be discovered as to the exact fate of the crew and passengers. Captain Bennett had with him, as mates on his last trip, John Thompson and Joseph Johnson, both experienced seamen, and the supposition is that the schooner, being new and stiff, was caught in a gale and 'turned turtle.' The craft was valued at $32,000, the cargo at $18,000, and there was also $10,000 in coin aboard with which to pay bills incurred in her construction. E. B. Deane and Mrs. Haughstead of San Francisco were associated with Captain Bennett in the ownership." (Wright, 1895, 228)

In *Pacific Graveyard*, by Jim Gibbs, the author says there was a story that the ship was sabotaged by the passengers, who escaped with a keg of gold, amounting to more than $10,000. Another story said that the barrel of coins was buried by an officer in the sands fifteen miles north of Coos Bay, after the ship had gone aground. (Gibbs, 1964, 204-205.)

Fred Lockley, the *Journal* man, met with Frank A.Collard of Florence in 1932, who told him the ship carried 25 souls, a crew of 10 men, with 15 passengers who were all mysteriously lost.

Mr. Esterbrook was a member of the crew of the *Peacock*, lost on the northern spit near the entrance of the Columbia, in 1839. (Lockley, *Oregon Journal*, 1932)

Oriental Junks

Tonquin Anchor

The marine editor, Lawrence Barber, writes about the sighting of a sunken vessel at Vancouver Island seen by divers from Portland in the summer of 1957. The underwater explorers, Tom Amerman and Dr. George W. Cottrell, were searching an area of Sydney inlet, for the *Tonquin*, on the coast of Vancouver Island. The expedition was diving in 40 to 75 foot depths where they uncovered a rusted cannon with a 4-inch caliber at seven and a half feet long, and other metal pieces from the unidentified wreck.

The mystery ship's hull was about 100 feet long covered with copper sheathing and fittings. A Canadian vessel was sent to recover the cannon and to return the ancient piece to Victoria, where it was put on display in the B.C. maritime museum.

Lt. Ed McFayden, curator of the museum, explained how a considerable amount of research was needed to identify the ship, since no records existed of a wreck at that location. (Barber, Oregonian, 1957)

An attempt to locate the sunken remains of the ship was conducted in 1983, by the Canadian Royal Military College, using sophisticated sub-bottom acoustic profile equipment, but without success.

Tonquin

The location of the *Tonquin* was known by a Catholic missionary from Hesquiot – Augustine J. Brabant. He had learned of the site from a Vancouver Island native, who placed it near Lennard Island, and close to the island village in Templar Channel. Many blankets were left floating on the water, after the explosion of Astor's ship, and gathered up by the people of the Sound, who passed these valuable coverings to their descendents. (Ruby and Brown, 1976, 139)

Diver Rod Palm has searched for the sunken remains of the *Tonquin* for 35 years, trying to solve Oregon's oldest maritime mystery. He was led to Vancouver Island after hearing a story that a crabber had snagged his net on an obstruction near Tofino. It turned out to be an 11- foot anchor, identical to that used on Astor's ship.

The ancient relic was laying exactly where oral histories described the sinking of the American ship. The design of the anchor was the same as those used on ships of the late 1700s. Blue beads were also found nearby, which were the most popular items of trade, among the coastal Indians. (Denson, *Oregonian*, 2003)

Isabella

The Hudson's Bay Company supply ship *Isabella* was abandoned on May 3, 1830 after Captain William Ryan, missed the channel into Cape Disappointment and grounded near Sand Island. The crew was able to unload most of the cargo during the next three weeks, which included blankets, cloth thread, pots and pans, tools muskets and 400 pounds of gingerbread.

It was a two-masted brig, about 90 feet long, with a 200 ton cargo capacity, constructed at the wharf of Fort Vancouver, and is the oldest shipwreck discovered at the mouth of the Columbia River.

A team of scientists from the National Park Service found the ship, just 30 feet below the surface of the river, after making a series of dives in August, 1987. The site was pinpointed in September 1986, by Daryl Hughes, a commercial fisherman from Chinook, after he snagged his net on the ship's remains. The shipwreck location was registered as an archaeological site with the State Archaeologist to protect it from fisherman and other possible explorers.

The team developed an electronic mapping system – Sonic High Accuracy Ranging and Positioning, to take measurements of the wreckage and to establish its exact location. The new system can be connected to a computer to produce video images of the shipwreck.

The wreckage proved to be a Colonial era ship, after pieces of wood and metal were analyzed in a laboratory. A hole 15 by 16 inches in the starboard side helped identify the vessel after the investigators read the ships log entry for May 9, 1830: "Cut a hole in the side to let the water out so that we could better get the cargo."

Another HBC supply ship, the *William & Ann*, was also lost on Clatsop Spit on March 11, 1829, but her remains have never been located.

Some of the Hudson's Bay Company's small craft operated along the coast, trading for pelts, like the *Cadboro*, which was built in London, and was sent with the *William & Ann* in 1827. The *Broughton* was built at the Fort and also, the *Vancouver* which was ready for coastal service by 1828.

John Hobson and Solomon Smith traveled to Nehalem to purchase a large case of drugs, from the Indians in 1848, that came ashore after the wreck of the *Vancouver*.

James Seeley White, diver and amateur archaeologist, has been investigating the old Fort Vancouver docks, the Hudson's Bay Company wharf site, for the National Park Service and has found ceramics where the wharf was constructed. (Oregonian, 1986 and (Cullimore, Oregonian, 1987. Also read Ch. 1, "Graveyard of the Pacific" in "Adventures of a Sea Hunter: In Search of Famous Shipwrecks" by James P. Delgado)

This anchor was recovered from the Columbia River in 1960, near the Fort Vancouver wharf, a quarter mile east of the Interstate, I-5 bridge. It is a Rogers Patent Small-Palm anchor made in England between 1815 and 1850, designed for a ship of a thousand tons. It could be from the British sloop Modeste, 18 guns, commanded by Thomas Baillie, visiting Fort Vancouver 1844-1845. (author photo)

Golden Quest

The Oregonian reported during the last days of July, 1989, on the efforts of a San Diego based salvage company to search Nehalem Bay for the remains of a lost Spanish galleon. The company, Golden Quest Inc., is led by Bill Warren, who has been on 50 salvage expeditions since 1976. In 1978, Mr Warren used Spectrographic Infrared Photography to locate the ship he believes is the *San Francisco Xavier*. It was one of many galleons that crossed the pacific between Manila and New Spain carrying silks, jewels, and Chinese porcelain, worth today an "estimated $500 million," Warren said.

After receiving a salvage permit, he planned to use a 20 person team to excavate the shipwreck; with historians, divers, and archaeologists. He was to begin searching with the RCV 150, an undersea electronic robot built by Honeywell Corporation, that uses three cameras; two video and one still, and claws that can pick up an artifact the size of a dime.

The company was unable to salvage the wreck site due to the necessary requirements from port authorities and the Army Corps of Engineers. (Francis, Oregonian, 1989)

Beeswax Wreck Project

A research team has been organized under the title of the "Beeswax Wreck Project" to conduct the first archaeological study of the shipwreck near Nehalem Bay State Park. The Project is supported by the Naga Research Group, a non-profit archaeological organization based in Hawaii. The group is led by Scot Williams, an archaeologist with the Natural Resources Conservation service in Olympia, Washington. He is joined by additional scientists in underwater archaeology and specialists in Chinese porcelain. The researchers are following the efforts of Eb Giesecke, also of Olympia, who has been studying the shipwreck for more than 50 years, and has interviewed Nehalem Bay residents since 1954.

The co-leader with Williams, is Julie Schablitsky an archaeologist from the University of Oregon. Her husband Robert Neyland, is head of the U. S. Navy's underwater archaeological unit in Washington, D. C.

Their studies have narrowed the identity of the ship, down to two galleons: the *Santo Christo de Burgos,* lost in 1693, and the *San Francisco Xavier*, which was reported missing in 1705.

A geophysicist, Sheldon Breiner, who has experience in other archaeological projects, has found five potential wreck sites offshore, but none on the beach. He was using a magnetometer, the instrument that detects irregularities in subsurface magnetic fields. He determined that all five anomalies on the seafloor were from ships, and one of the hits may be a cannon from the galleon.(Hill, Oregonian, 2007)

Winter 2007

Winter storms that hit the Oregon coast in 2007 uncovered a lost ship near Coos Bay, that turned out to be the *George L. Olson*, grounded at the north jetty on June 23, 1944. At first the schooner's identity was uncertain, but after Megan Harper of the Bureau of Land Management received a photograph of the Olson, the ship's identity was certain. The photo was taken in 1947 of a local man and his brothers on the shipwreck with "George L." on the hull. The lumber hauler was originally named the *Ryder*, a 223 foot wood-hulled schooner launched in 1917.

At Arch Cape, seventeen feet of sand eroded away revealing a pair of cannons, weighing 800 and 1000 pounds each, that could be additional pieces from the *USS Shark*, the survey ship that wrecked in 1846 near the Columbia River bar. The cannons were removed from the beach by State archaeologist Dennis Griffin, wrapped in burlap, and placed in freshwater tanks for preservation.

Loretta LeGuee picked up a 10 pound piece of beeswax, while beachcombing with Norman, her German shepherd, just south of Gold Beach in early December. Scott Williams, assistant state archaeologist for Washington, identified the block from a picture he received. It was unusual finding beeswax that far south, since "ocean currents off Oregon flow north, not south," Williams added. It was most likely from the Nehalem shore, and arrived by trade, conducted by the Indian tribes of the coast, instead of current drift.

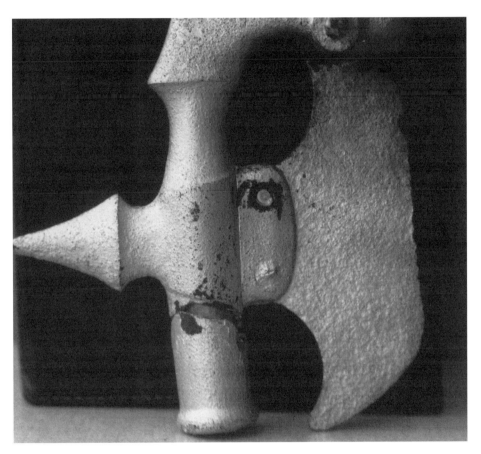

Artifact recovered from the mouth of the Nehalem River by Robert Nash and believed to be the head of a Spanish halberd from the late 17th century. (Ben Maxwell photo. Salem Public Library Historic Photograph Collection)

The article "Spanish Battle Ax Found by Diver off Nehalem Spit" was written by Eleanor Wimber, but the source and the date are unknown.

Robert Nash, of Everett, Washington, was scuba diving off the Nehalem spit, north of the north jetty, when he came across a rusty object, in 60 feet of water. The relic is believed by many to be the head of an ancient Spanish halberd, used in the 15th and 16th centuries. A piece of the long-handled weapon was recently sent to Shell Oil Company's laboratory in Texas, where a carbon-14 test, dated it to the latter part of the 17th century. The blade of the halberd is 6.5 inches from tip to tip, and would appear to be Spanish.

Gold recovered from the Columbia River!

Gold was sifted out of the sandy bottom at the mouth of the great river, as reported by Jim Gibbs, in his "Disaster Log of Ships" a most exciting discovery for the scuba diver, Robert Everett.

Everett was working beyond the breakers, just south of the Columbia searching for the remains of sunken ships when he suddenly came across an old hulk. He ran into rusted metal bunks and what he thought was the ship's stack, and then suddenly, he caught a glimpse of a dull brown metallic object. He quickly picked up a nearby shell, and began scraping until he exposed a bright yellow surface. It was gold! A solid gold ingot! Of course there must be more, he hoped. He set the gold bar in a sling and headed for the surface, to announce the discovery to his diving buddies.

The dive boat stayed over the wreck site, and Everett went down again – five times he surfaced with gold ingots, Spanish coins, and other relics. By nightfall the dive team had accumulated a small treasure, now laying in the bottom of their little boat.

Everett was convinced that the gold was from a Spanish wreck, lost in ancient times, and was covered by another more recent shipwreck, of modern design. This chance discovery of the gold ingot and Spanish coins proved it.

According to Harry Rieseberg, the famous diver and treasure hunter, Everett's day of underwater salvage netted him an amazing $60,000. (Gibbs, 1971, 41-43)

Gibbs also lists an unknown Spanish vessel, 1725 on Clatsop

Beach in his Appendix – Major Shipwrecks, from "Shipwrecks of the Pacific Coast" p. 273., and also "Pacific Graveyard" Gibbs, p. 278.

Unidentified Nehalem Ship

James Seeley White came across evidence of a shipwreck in Nehalem bay, in the spring of 1973. It was a formation of rocks that was a typical "ballast pattern" first seen by his diving buddy, Irv Jones near the south end of the bay.

They collected some ballast samples and delivered them to the Oregon Department of Geology, where they learned that the rocks were probably from Europe, but some came from Mexico.

The publication of the Department of Geology and Mineral Industries, the "Ore Bin," released the results of the examination of the rock samples, in the October 1975 issue and stated "that the Manzanita wreck was not a local vessel," since it carried ballast rock common to Europe, such as "gneiss and quartzite," and some rock which would have been gathered from the Mexican coast, like "dacite." The stones were beach rocks, according to Ralph Mason, as opposed to quarried rock.

Large cobble stones were used as ballast by Spanish ships of the 16th through the 18th centuries and during the same period, coarse gravel was employed as ballast by English merchantmen & warships.

They measured the ballast area - 30 feet long by 13 feet wide, which brought to mind the American Revolution "privateer schooner" acquired by the Royal Navy, through capture and purchase, that were a little longer than 70 feet, with a 50 foot keel, which would leave a ballast pattern of approximately 30 feet.

The divers then returned to the site and dug a trench through the ballast while searching for any other evidence, that would be associated with a shipwreck, such as ship timbers, metal fittings, or even an anchor, but they found nothing. Then they made a most exciting discovery – bricks! The ballast contained bricks, some with the word "Ravens," others were stamped with "WBI&Co," and some broken pieces with part of a word – "ottle."

About this time they received word that the vessel could

be the remains of the *Charles H. Merchant*, an American lumber schooner, wrecked at the Nehalem entrance in 1902, towed to this ballast discovery site and dynamited. White didn't believe it, but decided to do some more research at the library. None of the wrecks near the Nehalem River were known to be English – most of the of the wrecks occurred at the entrance, or on the beach. Most of these were not salvaged, and none of them seemed to connect to his ship.

Then they received information from Basil Saffer, Curator of the General Shale Museum of Ancient Brick, Johnson City, Tennessee, who said the bricks were made "not much before 1800."

From England came great news, in a letter from J. T. Kailofer, who identified the bricks as being manufactured in the village of Walbottle, near Newcastle upon the Tyne, sometime before 1840. He also included that there was a group of "merchant venturers" that were operating illegally from Newcastle, during the very period that the ship would have sailed along the Pacific coast. These privateers were most likely trading with the Indians, without a charter, since the crown had awarded this to the Hudson's Bay Company, and that "Ramsay, or Ramsey," was a common name in the Tyne area, near the border with Scotland. (White, 1982, "Epilogue" 171-174, and Oregon Journal, 1976)

"Map of the Department of the Columbia" 1881.

Appendix A

Vessels to the Northwest Coast 1819-1840
- Hubert Howe Bancroft

"Herewith is appended a list of such vessels as have come to my knowledge that are known to have touched on the Northwest Coast from 1819 to 1840. It has been made up of such fragmentary records as could be found, many of them neither official nor accurate. The files of Sandwich Island, newspapers were a useful source of information on this subject after 1836. The California archives also afforded some items not elsewhere appearing; and it is probable that others of the vessels named in the California annual lists – for which see another volume of this series – should be added to this, but there are no means of knowing which ones. Printed memoirs of the Oregon missionaries contain some names; the Hudson's Bay Company's archives others; while I have a few old log-books or fragments; and for the rest we are obliged to depend on the manuscript reminiscences of men who in those days went down to the sea in ships. I do not include in the list the Russian vessels plying each year between Sitka, Ross, and the Spanish ports of California, often extending their trips to Mexico, South America, Asia, or the islands; nor do I mention the whalers that visited the north Pacific in great numbers, and are recorded as touching in California and the Sandwich Islands; though, it is likely that some vessels of both these classes touched from time to time on the coast, between latitude 42 degrees and 55 degrees. I shall have occasion to present more details respecting many of the vessels and commanders here mentioned, in later chapters and volumes of this work. The list arranged chronologically is as follows:

1819-20. *Borneo*, George Clark, American ship; wrecked at Kaigan in January 1819.

Volunteer, James Bennett, Boston ship; carried crew of *Borneo* back to the Sandwich Islands.

Brutus, David Nye, Boston brig; made a trip to Alaska and probably down the coast.

Eagle, Thomas Meek, Boston ship; from Northwest Coast to China. All these items are taken from a sketch of Captain William Smith's life in the Boston *Daily Advertiser* and *Niles' Register*, xvii, 418.

1820 – A Japanese junk, laden with wax, cast away on Point Adams, according to Mr. Brooks.

1821 – *Arab*, American brig; trading on the coast. I have her original log, which lacks, however, both beginning and end. It is in this log that I find the following trading-vessels of this year:

Fredie, Stetson, Boston brig; arrived in August and went to Sandwich Islands.

Pedler, Meek, New York brig.

Sultan, consort of the *Fredie*.

Hamilton, Lascar, and *Mentor,* all Boston vessels; and two commanded by captains Post and Martin, perhaps identical with some of the preceding.

1823-5 – *Rob Roy*, Cross, Boston brig, owned by Bryant and Sturgis; trading on the coast, also probably in later years. Mentioned in the *Memoranda* of Henry A. Peirce.

1824 et seq. – *Herald,* Hammatt, owned by Bryant and Sturgis.

Triton, Bryant, owned by Bryant and Sturgis.

Sultan, Allen, owned by Bryant and Sturgis.

Convoy, McNeill, owned by Josiah Marshall.

1825-8 – *Griffon*, M. T. Peirce, Boston brig, owned by Bryant and Sturgis; engaged in trade on the Northwest Coast. Henry A. Peirce, brother of the captain, was on board, and gives a full account of the trip in his *Memoranda*.

1827 – *Cadboro*, Simpson, British schooner, from Columbia River; in California in December.

1828-30 – *Volunteer*, Seth Barker, owned by Bryant and Sturgis.

Active, Cotting or Cotton, owned by William Baker and Company.

Louisa, Martin, owned by William Baker and Company.

Owyhee, Kelly, owned by Josiah Marshall.

1828 – *William and Ann*, Hudson's Bay Company's vessel; wrecked inside the Columbia bar.

1829-30 – *Owyhee*, Dominis, Boston ship; traded in Columbia River.

Convoy, Thompson; with the *Owyhee*.

1830 – *Isabella*, Hudson's Bay Company's brig; castaway in Columbia River.

1831 – A Japanese junk wrecked on Queen Charlotte Island, according to Mr. Brooks.

1831-32 – *Dryad*, English brig; in California from the Columbia River both years.

1833 – Another Japanese wreck near Cape Flattery.

1834 – *Llama* or *Lama*, William O'Neill, Hudson's Bay Company's brig; in California for supplies, from Columbia river.

May Dacre, Lambert, American brig; in Columbia River for trade and salmon.

Europa, Allen, Boston trader on the coast, according to Kelley's *Memoir*.

1835 – *May Dacre*, still in the river; Wyeth owner and agent.

Ganymede, Eales, Hudson's Bay Company's bark; in Columbia River.

Dryad, Keplin, left Columbia River for Sandwich Islands.

1836 – *Joseph Peabody*, Moore; arrived at Honolulu from Northwest Coast and Kaigan, sailing for New York.

- *Columbia*, Darby, Hudson's Bay Company's bark; at Honolulu from Columbia River,. At Honolulu again under Captain Royal in December, and sailed for London.

Nereid, Royal, Hudson's Bay Company's bark; arrived at Honolulu from England, and arrived at Columbia river in August.

Llama, McNeill; in Columbia River and at Kaigan.

Europa, William Winkworth; from Honolulu to Northwest Coast and to Monterey.

Loriot, Nye, Blinn, and Bancroft successively; American trader, on special service in Columbia River, California, and Sandwich Islands.

Convoy, Bancroft and later Burch, American brig; from Kaigan to Honolulu and back.

La Grange, Snow, Boston ship; at Honolulu from Kaigan and other ports on Northwest Coast.

Beaver, Holm, Hudson's Bay Company's steamer; in Columbia River, the first steamer to visit the coast.

1837 – *Llama*, Bancroft, Sangster, Brotchie, and McNeill; from Columbia River to Honolulu and California.

Nereid; still in Columbia River.

Cadboro, William Brotchie, Hudson's Bay Company's schooner; made a trip from Columbia River to California.

Loriot, Bancroft; from Columbia River to California and Sandwich Islands; also a trip to Mazatlan under Captain Handley.

Sumatra, Duncan, English bark, carried missionaries from Honolulu to Columbia River.

Hamilton, S. Barker, American ship; trading trip from Honolulu to the Northwest Coast.

Diana, William S. Hinkley, American brig; carried missionaries from Honolulu to Columbia River; trip to California; named changed to *Kamamalu.*

Sulphur, Edward Belcher, H. B. M. ship; on an exploring voyage round the world; spent a week in Nootka Sound.

Starling, H. Kellett, H. B. M. Exploring schooner; in company with the *Sulphur.*

1838 – *Llama*, Bancroft, later Robinson and Perrier; hunting and trading trips to California and Sandwich Islands.

Nereid, Brotchie; at Honolulu from Columbia River, also in California.

Cadboro, Robbins; in California from Columbia River.

Joseph Peabody; engaged in fur-trade, according to Kelley's *Memoir.*

Columbia, Humphries; from England to Columbia River and return via Sandwich Islands.

1839 – *Nereid*, Brotchie; trip from the Columbia river to the Islands and back.

Vancouver, Duncan, Hudson's Bay Company's bark; from London to Columbia River and back to Honolulu.

Thomas Perkins, Varney; left Sandwich Islands for Northwest Coast to trade.

Joseph Peabody, Dominis; trading on Alaska coast and perhaps farther south.

Sulphur, Belcher; in Columbia River, July to September.

Starling, Kellett; with the preceding.

1840 – *Columbia*, Humphries; in California, Sandwich Islands, and Columbia River.

Forager, Thompson, English brig; left Honolulu for Columbia River and California.

Lausanne, Spaulding, American ship; in Columbia River, California, and Sandwich Islands; settlers and missionaries.

Maryland, Couch, Boston brig; in Columbia River, trading for salmon.

(Bancroft, 1884, vol. 1, 340-342)

Appendix B

Japanese wrecks on the Pacific coast / European and American
- Hubert Howe Bancroft

"One at Acapulco in 1617; Bantam Islands, 1613; adrift, 1685; Kamchatka, 1694, 1710, 1729, and 1812, where several other wrecks are alluded to by Muller; Aleutian Isles, 1782; stranded junk crew of fifteen rescued by Krusenstern, 1804; near Sitka, 1805; adrift, 1813, adrift off Santa Barbara, 1815; a junk laden with wax was thrown upon Point Adams in 1820; one wrecked on Queen Charlotte Island in 1831; Hawaiian Islands, 1832; near cape Flattery, 1833; adrift west of the Hawaiian Isles, 1839; South Sea Isle, 1841; Mexico, 1845; St Peter Isle, 1845; Stapleton Island, 1847; adrift, 1847, 1848, and 1850; Atka Island, 1851; adrift, 1852, and 1853; near Cedros Island, Lower California, 1853; adrift near Hawaiian Isles, 1854; adrift, 1855; Ladrone Islands and Cedros, 1856; two adrift in 1858; one at Ocean Island, and one at Book Island in 1859; adrift, 1862, two; Baker Island, 1863; Providence Island, 1864; Aleutian Isles, 1869; adrift, 1870, and in 1871 two; Atka, 1871; adrift, 1873; at Alaska, Hawaii, Petropaulski, adrift below San Diego, Nootka Sound, were Japanese wrecks at various dates; adrift, 1875 and 1876. Charles Wolcott Brooks in an able and comprehensive *brochure* on the *Japanese Wrecks , Stranded and picked up Adrift in the North Pacific Ocean,* prepared for the purpose of illustrating early migrations, made out a list, and at various times I have learned of a few additional. Horace Davis in his ethnological speculations, *Record of Japanese Vessels driven upon the Northwest Coast of America,* gives a list of such wrecks as came to his knowledge, which was one of the chief sources of Mr Brooks' information. In the *Polynesian* are mentioned three Japanese picked up near the mouth of the Columbia in 1829, and a junk adrift in 1846, not catalogued by Brooks. Victor, *Or. And Wash.,* 51, says in the sands round the mouth of the Columbia pieces of wax, washed up during violent storms, were found for years.

As for European and American wrecks on the Northwest Coast we have what was supposed to be a Spanish vessel from Manila in 1772 – *Kelley*, in *Thornton's Or. Hist.*, MS., 87; *Oregon Spectator*, Jan. 21, 1847 – with a cargo of beeswax cast ashore on the northern side of the entrance to the Columbia; in 1828, at the entrance of the Columbia, the *William and Ann*; in 1830, at the entrance to the Columbia, the *Isabel*; in 1841, at the entrance to the Columbia, the U. S. ship *Peacock;* in Sept. 1846, at the entrance of the Columbia, the U. S. schooner *Shark*; in 1848, at the entrance of the Columbia, the bark *Vancouver;* in 1849, at mouth of the Columbia, the brig *Josephine*; likewise elsewhere and at another time, *Silva de Grace,* and *James Warren,* the latter fifty miles south of Killamook; in 1851-2, at the mouth of the Umpqua, brig *Caleb Curtis*, and schooner *Nassau*; in 1852, near Killamook, schooner *Juliet* on Vancouver Island, brig *Eagle*; in 1853, barks *Oriole, T. Merithew,* and *Mendora*, and brig *Vandalia* on the Columbia bar; in 1854, at mouth of Columbia, steam-tug *Fire-Fly*; steam-boat *Castle*, boiler exploded; in 1855, near mouth of Umpqua, schooner *Loo Choo*; in 1856, at Coos Bay, brig *Quadratus*; brig *Fawn* bound for Umpqua River, went ashore near the mouth of the Siuslaw; at Port Orford the *Iowa* and *Francisco;* in 1857, brig *Jackson* and bark *New World* grounded at Coos Bay; bark *Desdemona* wrecked on Columbia bar. (Bancroft, vol. 2, 532-533.)

Bibliography

Aikens, C. Melvin, *Archaeology of Oregon*, Portland, Oregon, U. S. Department of Interior, Bureau of Land Management, 1993.

Ames, Kenneth M. and Herbert D. G. Maschner, *Peoples of the Northwest Coast: Their Archaeology and Pre-History* New York, Thames and Hudson, 1999.

Bancroft, Hubert Howe *History of the Northwest Coast*, San Francisco, California, A. L. Bancroft, Publishers, 1884.

Battaile, Connie Hopkins *The Oregon Book: Information A to Z*, Newport, Oregon, Saddle Mountain Press, 1998.

Bawlf, Samuel *The Secret Voyage of Sir Francis Drake*, New York, Walker & Company, 2003.

Becham, Stephen Dow *Oregon Indians: Voices From Two Centuries* Corvallis, Oregon, Oregon State University Press, 2006.

Carey, Charles Henry *History of Oregon*, Chicago-Portland, The Pioneer Historical Publishing Company, 1922.

Carey, Charles Henry *General History of Oregon*, Portland, Oregon, Binfords & Mort, Publishers, 1971.

Clarke, S. A. *Pioneer Days of Oregon History*, Portland, Oregon, J. K. Gill Company, 1905.

Cook, Warren *Flood Tide of Empire: Spanish and the Pacific Northwest, 1543-1819*, New Haven, Ct., Yale University Press, 1973.

Comerford, Jane Ann *At the Foot of the Mountain*, Portland, Oregon, Dragonfly Press, 2004.

Corning, Howard McKinley *Dictionary of Oregon History*, Portland, Oregon, Binfords & Mort, Publishers, 1989.

Cotton, S. J. *Stories of Nehalem*, Chicago, Il., M. A. Donahue & Company, 1915.

Cox, Ross *The Columbia River*, edited by Edgar I. Stewart and Jane R. Stewart, Norman, Oklahoma, University of Oklahoma Press, 1957.

Delgado, James P. *Adventures of a Sea Hunter: In Search of Famous Shipwrecks*, Vancouver B. C., Douglas & McIntyre, 2004.

Drawson, Maynard C. *Treasures of the Oregon Country*, Salem, Oregon, Dee Publishing Co., 1973.

Du Pratz, Antoine Simon Le Page, *The History of Louisiana*, London, T. Becket, 1774.

Evans, Elwood *History of the Pacific Northwest – Oregon and Wash-

ington Portland, Oregon, North Pacific History Company, 1889.

Franchere, Gabriel *Adventures at Astoria, 1810-1814*, translated & edited by Hoyt C. Franchere, Norman, Oklahoma, University of Oklahoma Press, 1967.

Gibbon, John Murray *Steel of Empire: The Romantic History of the Canadian Pacific, the Northwest Passage of Today*, New York, The Bobbs-Merrill Company, Publishers, 1935.

Gibbs, James A. *Pacific Graveyard: A Narrative of Shipwrecks where the Columbia Meets the Pacific Ocean*, Portland, Oregon, Binfords & Mort, Publishers, 1964.

Gibbs – *Oregon's Salty Coast*, Seattle, Washington, Superior Publishing Company, 1978.

Gibbs – *Shipwrecks of the Pacific Coast*, Portland, Oregon, Binfords & Mort, Publishing, 1971.

Gibbs – *Disaster Log of Ships* Seattle, Washington, Superior Publishing Company, 1971.

Gibson, James R. *Otter Skins, Boston Ships, and China Goods: The Maritime Fur Trade of the Northwest Coast, 1785-1841*, Seattle, Washington, University of Washington Press, 1992.

Giesecke, E. W. *Beeswax, Teak and Castaways: Searching for Oregon's Lost Protohistoric Asian Ship* Tillamook, Oregon, Nehalem Valley Historical Society, 2007.

Gray, W. H. *A History of Oregon, 1792-1849, Drawn from Personal Observation and Authentic Information* Portland, Oregon, Harris & Holman, 1870.

Green, Frank L. *Captains, Curates, and Cockneys: The English in the Pacific Northwest* Tacoma, Washington, Washington State Historical Society, 1981.

Gulick, Bill *Roadside History of Oregon* Missoula, Montana, Mountain Press Publishing Company, 2002.

Hampden, John *Francis Drake Privateer: Contemporary Narratives and Documents* University of Alabama Press, 1972.

Hanna, Warren L. *Lost Harbor: The Controversy over Drake's California Anchorage* Berkeley, California, University of California Press, 1979.

Hayes, Derek *Historical Atlas of the Pacific Northwest: Maps of Exploration and Discovery* Seattle, Washington, Sasquatch Books, 1999.

Hirt, Paul W. *Terra Pacifica: People and Place in the Northwest States and Western Canada* Pullman, Washington, Washington State University Press, 1998.

Horner, John B. *Days and Deeds in the Oregon Country* Portland, Oregon, The J. K. Gill Company, 1929.

Howay, F. W. *A List of Trading Vessels in the Maritime Fur Trade, 1785-1825* edited by Richard A. Pierce, The Limestone Press, Ontario, 1973.

Hult, Ruby El *Lost Mines and Treasures of the Pacific Northwest* Portland, Oregon, Binfords & Mort, Publishers, 1957.

Hult – *Treasure Hunting Northwest* Portland, Oregon, Binfords & Mort, 1971.

Irving, Washington *Astoria* New York, G. P. Putnam's Sons, 1897.

Jackson, John C. *Children of the Fur Trade: Forgotten Metis of the Pacific Northwest* Missoula, Montana, Mountain Press Publishing, 1995.

Jameson, W. C. *Buried Treasures of the Pacific Northwest: Secret Indian Mines, Lost Outlaw Hoards, and Stolen Payroll Coins* Little Rock, Arkansas, August House Publishers Inc., 1995.

Judson, Katherine Berry, M. A. *Early Days in Old Oregon* Portland, Oregon, Binfords & Mort, Publishers, 1944.

Larsell, O. *The Doctor in Oregon: A Medical History* Portland, Oregon, published by Binfords & Mort for the Oregon Historical Society, 1947.

Laut, Agnes C. *Pioneers of the Pacific Coast: A Chronicle of Sea Rovers and Fur Traders* 1915.

Lee, D. and J. H. Frost *Ten Years in Oregon* New York, J. Collard, Printer, 1844.

Lonsdale, Adrian L. and H. R. Kaplan *A Guide to Sunken Ships in American Waters* Arlington, Virginia, Compass Publications Inc., 1964.

Lyman, William Denison *The Columbia River: Its History, Its Myths, Its Scenery, Its Commerce* Portland, Oregon, Binfords & Mort, Publishers, 1963.

Malloy, Mary. "Boston Men on the Northwest Coast: The American Maritime Fur Trade, 1788-1844." Ontario: The Timestone Press, 1998.

Marshall, Don *Oregon Shipwrecks* Portland, Oregon, Binford & Mort, Publishers, 1984.

Menzies, Gavin *1421: The Year China Discovered America* New York, William Morrow, 2002.

Mertz, Henriette *Pale Ink: Two Ancient Records of Chinese Exploration in America* Chicago, Ill. 1953.

Miller, Emma Gene *Clatsop County, Oregon: Its History, Legends, and Industries* Portland, Oregon, Binfords & Mort, 1958.

McDonald, Lucille *Coast Country: A History of Southwest Washington* Portland, Oregon, Binfords & Mort, 1966.

Moody, Skye *Washed Up: The Curious Journeys of Flotsam and Jetsam* Seattle, Washington, Sasquatch Books, 2006.

Morris, Elizabeth & Mark *Moon Handbooks: Coastal Oregon* Emeryville, California, Avalon Travel Publishing, 2004.

Nokes, J. Richard *Columbia's River: The Voyages of Robert Gray, 1787-1793* Tacoma, Washington, Washington State Historical Society, 1991.

Orcutt, Ada M. *Tillamook: Land of Many Waters* Portland, Oregon, Binfords & Mort, Publishers, 1951.

Pethick, Derek *First Approaches to the Northwest Coast* Seattle and London, University of Washington Press, 1979.

Ranck, Glenn N. *Legends and Traditions of Northwest History* Vancouver, Washington, American Printing and Stationary Company, 1907.

Rogers, Thomas H. *Beeswax and Gold: A Story of the Pacific A.D. 1700* Portland, Oregon, The J. K. Gill Company, Publishers, 1929.

Ronda, James P. *Astoria and Empire* Lincoln & London, University of Nebraska Press, 1990.

Ross, Alexander *Adventures of the First Settlers on the Oregon or Columbia River"* edited by Milo Milton Quaife, New York, The Citadel Press, 1969.

Ruby, Robert H. and John A. Brown *Indians of the Pacific Northwest, A History* Norman, Oklahoma, University of Oklahoma Press, 1981.

Ruby and Brown – *The Chinook Indians: Traders on the Lower Columbia River* Norman, and London, University of Oklahoma Press, 1976.

Ruby and Brown – *Indian Slavery in the Pacific Northwest* Spokane, Washington, The Arthur H. Clark Company, 1993.

Sauter, John and Bruce Johnson, *Tillamook Indians of the Oregon Coast* Portland, Oregon, Binfords & Mort, Publishers, 1974.

Schafer, Joseph *A History of the Pacific Northwest* New York, The Macmillan Company, 1905.

Schurz, William Lytle *The Manila Galleon* New York, E. P. Dutton, 1939.

Seaman, N. G. *Indian Relics of the Pacific Northwest* Portland, Oregon, Binford & Mort, 1967.

Snyder, Eugene E. *Early Portland: Stump-Town Triumphant* Portland, Oregon, Binford & Mort, Publishing, 1970.

Swan, James G. *The Northwest Coast, or Three Years Residence in*

Washington Territory New York, Harper & Brothers, Publishers, 1857.

Townsend, John Kirk *Narrative of a Journey Across the Rocky Mountains to the Columbia River*, introduced and annotation by George A. Jobanek, Corvallis, Oregon, Oregon State University Press, 1999.

Victor, Mrs. Frances Fuller *All Over Oregon and Washington* San Francisco, printed by John H. Carmany & Co., 1872.

Vaughn, Warren *Till Broad Daylight: A History of Early Settlement in Oregon's Tillamook County* Wallowa, Oregon, Bear Creek Press, 2004.

Walker, Dale L. *Pacific Destiny: The Three Century Journey to the Oregon Country* New York, A Tom Doherty Associates Book, 2000.

Webber, Bert and Margie *Amazing True Tales of Wrecked Japanese Junks* Medford, Oregon, Webb Research Group, Publishers, 1999.

Webber, Bert *Wrecked Japanese Junks Adrift in the North Pacific Ocean* Fairfield, Washington, Ye Galleon Press, 1984.

Wheeler, Eugene D. and Robert E. Kallman *Shipwrecks, Smugglers & Maritime Mysteries* Ventura, California, Pathfinder Publishing, 1986.

White, James Seeley *The Spells of Lamazee: An Historical Novel of the Pacific Northwest Coast* Breitenbush Publications, Portland, Oregon, 1982.

Wilkes, Charles *Narrative of the United States Exploring Expedition During the Years, 1838, 1839, 1840, 1841, 1842* Philadelphia, Lee & Blanchard, 1845.

Winther, Oscar Osburn *The Great Northwest: A History* New York, Alfred A. Knopf, 1949.

Woodger, Elin and Brandon Toropov *Encyclopedia of the Lewis & Clark Expedition* New York, Checkmark Books, 2004.

Wright, E. W. *Lewis and Dryden's Marine History of the Pacific Northwest* Portland, Oregon, Lewis & Dryden Print Co., 1895.

Yenne, Bill *The Missions of California* San Diego, California, Thunder Bay Press, 2004.

Other Sources:

Archaeology of The Dalles-Deschutes Region by W. Duncan Strong, W. Egbert Schenck, and Julian H. Steward, University of California Publications in American Archaeology and Ethnology" vol. 29 no. 1, University of California Press, Berkeley, California,

1930.

Astorian Adventure: The Journal of Alfred Seton 1811-1815 edited by Robert F. Jones, Fordham University Press, New York, 1993.

Astorians Who Became Permanent Settlers by J. Neilson Barry, Washington Historical quarterly, 24 October 1933.

Boone Family Reminiscences by Eva Emery Dye, Oregon Historical Quarterly, vol. 42, March-December 1941.

Chinese porcelains from site 35-TI-1, Netarts Sand Spit, Tillamook County, Oregon, by Herbert K. Beals, and Harvey Steele, Department of Anthropology, University of Oregon, 1981.

Chinook Texts by Franz Boas, Smithsonian Institution, 1894.

Diary of Rev. George Gary by Charles Henry Carey, Oregon Historical Quarterly, vol. 24, 1923.

Discovery of 17ᵗʰ Century Coins Renews Local Interest in Lost Treasures of Spanish Main The North Tillamook County News, April 17, 1936.

Final Report, Fort Vancouver Excavations by Louis R. Caywood, Archaeologist, 1955.

Glimpses of Early Days in Oregon by Mrs. C. M. Cartwright, Oregon Historical Quarterly, vol. 4, 1903.

History of the Expedition of Captains Lewis and Clark, 1804-5-6 reprinted from the edition of 1814, with Introduction and Index by James K. Hosmer, A. C. McClurg & Co., Chicago, 1903.

How Many Treasures Are Buried Here? The Nehalem Bay Fishwrapper, September 21, 1978.

Ilwaco's Gold Mystery by Robert Nash, in "Frontier Times" December-January 1967.

Japanese Wrecks, Stranded and Picked up Adrift in the North Pacific Ocean by Charles Wolcott Brooks, 1875.

Messages in Beeswax From a Missing Galleon by Ben Maxwell "True West" August 1961.

National Geographic September, 1990.

Neah-kah-nie Mountain of Dreams by Curt Beckham, "Oregon Coast" November-December, 1990.

Nehalem Tillamook Tales as told by Clara Pearson, Melville Jacobs, editor, Oregon State University Press, Corvallis, Oregon, 1990.

New Light on the Early History of the Greater Northwest: The Manuscript Journals of Alexander Henry and David Thompson, 1799-1814 Elliot Coues, editor, first published in 1897.

Oregon Native Son and Historical Magazine Portland, Oregon, Native Son Pub. Co., 1899-1901.

Physical Evidence of shipwrecks on the Oregon coast in prehistory by Alison Stenger, "Screenings" The Oregon Archaeological Society Newsletter vol. 54 no. 8, August 2005.

Record of Japanese Vessels Driven Upon the North-West Coast of America and its Outlying Islands by Horace Davis, printed by Charles Hamilton, Worcester, Mass., 1872.

Soft Gold: The Fur Trade and Cultural Exchange on the Northwest Coast of America by Thomas Vaughn, Portland, Oregon, Oregon Historical Society, 1982.

Tales of the Neahkahnie Treasure Wayne Jensen, Tillamook County Pioneer Museum, 2nd printing, Tillamook, Oregon, 1991.

The Beeswax Ship Tillamook Headlight August 29, 1895.

The Definitive Journals of Lewis & Clark Gary E. Moulton, editor, vol. 6, "Down the Columbia River to Fort Clatsop," University of Nebraska Press, Lincoln and London, 2002.

The Wax of Nehalem Beach by O. F. Stafford, Oregon Historical Quarterly vol. IX, March-December 1908.

Teak From Wreck Sold About County Headlight Herald, February 22, 1924.

Tillamook Memories Tillamook Pioneer Association, Tillamook, Oregon, 1972.

Voyage of the East Indiaman Phoenix by Clarence Andrews, Washington Historical Quarterly, vol. 23, no. 1, January 1932.

Oregonian

"All About the Beeswax of Nehalem Beach" by O. F. Stafford, January 26, 1908.

"Anchor Found Off Vancouver Island May Belong to Ship Lost in 1811" by Bryan Denson, September 28, 2003.

"Ancient Spanish Coins Found Near Illahe: Silver Dated in 1700s Believed Lost by Visiting Miner" March 12, 1933.

"'Beeswax Ship' Researchers Want to Separate Legend From Truth" by Richard L. Hill, Oregonian, 2007.

"Beeswax and Lost Treasure" by Ben Maxwell, March, 8, 1953.

"Buried Treasure Chest of Neah-Kah-Nie Lures Gold Seekers" by Hope Beatrice Price, August 29, 1926.

"California TV Crew Shoots Treasure Story Linked With Legend of Neahkahnie Rocks" September 3, 1957.

"Clackamas Indian Grave Yields Buttons of Haitian Soldier" by C. Corbly Church, August 12, 1928.

"Divers feel confident shipwreck is Isabella" by Don Cullimore, August 26, 1987.

"Galleon Hunt So Far Finds Red Tape" by Mike Francis, July 26, 1989.

"Gold Piece Spaded Up at Ilwaco Revives Hidden Treasure Legend" March 30, 1936.

"Huge, Rusted Anchor Seen As Link To Legendary Lost Treasure Ship" by Stan Allyn, December 4, 1961.

"Identity of Sunken Vessel in B. C. Cove Unsettled" by Lawrence Barber, November 29, 1957.

"Indian burial grounds hold coin of China" John Guernsey, January 16, 1977.

"Lost Indian Mine of Tillamook Country" by Ellis Lucia, August 30, 1953.

"Lure of Fabled Rich Neahkahnie Treasure" by Alice Day Pratt, June 30, 1929.

"Mountain of Dreams and Dust" by Ron Petichord, Northwest Magazine section, March 31, 1968.

"Neah-Kah-Nie Mountain Summer Resorts Abound In Attractions for Vacationists" by Hal E. Hoss, June 17, 1917.

"Neah-Kah-Nie Treasure" by Edward M. Miller, September 19, 1932.

"Old Shipwrecks Bell Would Ring Diver's Chimes" by John Snell, August 24, 1987.

"Pirate Gold of Three Rocks Beach" by Eb Giesecke, Northwest Magazine section, November 25, 1956.

"Porcelain Findings-Mysteries Mount" by Bethanye McNichol, March 25, 1993.

"Plans Laid to Raise Fabled Ship in Sand" August 1, 1929.

"Researchers look to past to unravel Columbia River shipwreck mystery" December 19, 1986.

"Romance of Neah-Kah-Nie Mountain" by Lewis M. Head, September 26, 1909.

"The Buried Nehalem Treasure" May 29, 1890.

"The Case of the Shipwrecked Spaniard" by Eb Giesecke, February 11, 1959.

"The Legend of the Nehalem Beeswax Ship", Richard L. Hill, April 4, 2001.

"The Mountian's Golden Secret" by Ellis Lucia, American Weekly section, September 4, 1955.

"Treasure Found On Beach: Large Bills in Bottle" February 27, 1939.

"Treasure Hunt Revived" Oregonian, March 15, 1915.

"Treasure Map of Neah-Kah-Nie Mountain Recalls Stories of Pirate

Adventures" November 7, 1926.

"Unknown shipwreck bared by low tide at Siletz Bay" by Stan Allyn, February 6, 1972.

Oregon Journal

"Beach Comber Finds $300 Cash" March 6, 1939.

"Did Negro Pirate Once Terrorize Our Indians?" April 26, 1931.

"Impressions and Observations of the Journal Man" by Fred Lockely, June 20, 1924.

"Impressions and Observations of the Journal Man" by Fred Lockley, November 21, 1932.

"Indian Girl Plays Hooky; Finds $520 in Gold Pieces" March, 1939.

"Nehalem's Mysterious Redhead" by James Seeley White, Northwest Living section, July 12, 1976.

"Pacific Northwest – Treasure Tale Retold" February 14, 1932.

"Pair of Carved Stone Heads Revives Indian Tradition" November 24, 1912.

"Pirate or Merchantman" Fred Lockley, August 11, 1929.

"Treasure Hunters Seek Legendary Pirate Gold of Neahkahnie Area" by Olive Brunson, November 16, 1947.

"Treasure trove buried in Oregon Coast? By Eve Muss, March 12, 1977.

Additional Reading

"A Fool's Gold: A Story of Ancient Spanish Treasure, Two Pounds of Pot, and the Young Lawyer Almost Left Holding the Bag" by Bill Merritt, Bloomsbury Publishing, New York, 2006.

"Pirates of the Pacific Coast" by Achilles Massahos, Brian Benson, Kathleen Seligman, Michael O'Shaughnessy, and the Unknown Mariner, Lulu, Newport, Oregon, 2006.

"Slave Wives of the Nehalem" by Claire Warner Churchill.

Index